Refugees

Mike Venettone

Immigration to North America

Refugees

Mike Venettone

Senior Consulting Editor Stuart Anderson
former Associate Commissioner for Policy and Planning,
U.S. Citizenship and Immigration Services

Introduction by Marian L. Smith, Historian,
U.S. Citizenship and Immigration Services

Introduction by Peter A. Hammerschmidt,
former First Secretary, Permanent Mission of Canada to the United Nations

MASON CREST
PHILADELPHIA

Mason Crest
450 Parkway Drive, Suite D
Broomall, PA 19008
www.masoncrest.com

©2017 by Mason Crest, an imprint of National Highlights, Inc.

Printed and bound in the United States of America.

CPSIA Compliance Information: Batch #INA2016.
For further information, contact Mason Crest at 1-866-MCP-Book.

First printing
1 3 5 7 9 8 6 4 2

Library of Congress Cataloging-in-Publication Data

on file at the Library of Congress
ISBN: 978-1-4222-3681-9 (hc)
ISBN: 978-1-4222-8098-0 (ebook)

Immigration to North America series ISBN: 978-1-4222-3679-6

Table of Contents

KEY ICONS TO LOOK FOR:

 Words to Understand: These words with their easy-to-understand definitions will increase the reader's understanding of the text, while building vocabulary skills.

 Sidebars: This boxed material within the main text allows readers to build knowledge, gain insights, explore possibilities, and broaden their perspectives by weaving together additional information to provide realistic and holistic perspectives.

 Research Projects: Readers are pointed toward areas of further inquiry connected to each chapter. Suggestions are provided for projects that encourage deeper research and analysis.

 Text-Dependent Questions: These questions send the reader back to the text for more careful attention to the evidence presented there.

 Series Glossary of Key Terms: This back-of-the book glossary contains terminology used throughout this series. Words found here increase the reader's ability to read and comprehend higher-level books and articles in this field.

The Changing Face of the United States

Marian L. Smith, Historian
U.S. Citizenship and Immigration Services

Americans commonly assume that immigration today is very different than immigration of the past. The immigrants themselves appear to be unlike immigrants of earlier eras. Their language, their dress, their food, and their ways seem strange. At times people fear too many of these new immigrants will destroy the America they know. But has anything really changed? Do new immigrants have any different effect on America than old immigrants a century ago? Is the American fear of too much immigration a new development? Do immigrants really change America more than America changes the immigrants? The very subject of immigration raises many questions.

In the United States, immigration is more than a chapter in a history book. It is a continuous thread that links the present moment to the first settlers on North American shores. From the first colonists' arrival until today, immigrants have been met by Americans who both welcomed and feared them. Immigrant contributions were always welcome—on the farm, in the fields, and in the factories. Welcoming the poor, the persecuted, and the "huddled masses" became an American principle. Beginning with the original Pilgrims' flight from religious persecution in the 1600s, through the Irish migration to escape starvation in the 1800s, to the relocation of Central Americans seeking refuge from civil wars in the 1980s and 1990s, the United States has considered itself a haven for the destitute and the oppressed.

But there was also concern that immigrants would not adopt American ways, habits, or language. Too many immigrants might overwhelm America. If so, the dream of the Founding Fathers for United States government and society would be destroyed. For this reason, throughout American history some have argued that limiting or ending immigration is our patriotic duty. Benjamin Franklin feared there were so many German immigrants in Pennsylvania the Colonial Legislature would begin speaking German. "Progressive" leaders of the early 1900s feared that immigrants who could not read and understand the English language were not only exploited by "big business," but also served as the foundation for "machine politics" that undermined the U.S. Constitution. This theme continues today, usually voiced by those who bear no malice toward immigrants but who want to preserve American ideals.

Have immigrants changed? In colonial days, when most colonists were of English descent, they considered Germans, Swiss, and French immigrants as different. They were not "one of us" because they spoke a different language. Generations later, Americans of German or French descent viewed Polish, Italian, and Russian immigrants as strange. They were not "like us" because they had a different religion, or because they did not come from a tradition of constitutional government. Recently, Americans of Polish or Italian descent have seen Nicaraguan, Pakistani, or Vietnamese immigrants as too different to be included. It has long been said of American immigration that the latest ones to arrive usually want to close the door behind them.

It is important to remember that fear of individual immigrant groups seldom lasted, and always lessened. Benjamin Franklin's anxiety over German immigrants disappeared after those immigrants' sons and daughters helped the nation gain independence in the Revolutionary War. The Irish of the mid-1800s were among the most hated immigrants, but today we all wear green on St. Patrick's Day. While a century ago it was feared that Italian and other Catholic immigrants would vote as directed by the Pope, today that controversy is only a vague memory. Unfortunately, some ethnic groups continue their efforts to earn acceptance. The African

Americans' struggle continues, and some Asian Americans, whose families have been in America for generations, are the victims of current anti-immigrant sentiment.

Time changes both immigrants and America. Each wave of new immigrants, with their strange language and habits, eventually grows old and passes away. Their American-born children speak English. The immigrants' grandchildren are completely American. The strange foods of their ancestors—spaghetti, baklava, hummus, or tofu—become common in any American restaurant or grocery store. Much of what the immigrants brought to these shores is lost, principally their language. And what is gained becomes as American as St. Patrick's Day, Hanukkah, or Cinco de Mayo, and we forget that it was once something foreign.

Recent immigrants are all around us. They come from every corner of the earth to join in the American Dream. They will continue to help make the American Dream a reality, just as all the immigrants who came before them have done.

Welcome to the
United States
A Guide for New
Immigrants

UNITED STATES OF AMERICA   Department of Homeland Security
PERMANENT RESIDENT CARD

UNITED STATES OF AME

We recommend you use this enve
protect your new card.

The Changing Face of Canada

Peter A. Hammerschmidt
former First Secretary, Permanent Mission of Canada to the United Nations

Throughout Canada's history, immigration has shaped and defined the very character of Canadian society. The migration of peoples from every part of the world into Canada has profoundly changed the way we look, speak, eat, and live. Through close and distant relatives who left their lands in search of a better life, all Canadians have links to immigrant pasts. We are a nation built by and of immigrants.

Two parallel forces have shaped the history of Canadian immigration. The enormous diversity of Canada's immigrant population is the most obvious. In the beginning came the enterprising settlers of the "New World," the French and English colonists. Soon after came the Scottish, Irish, and Northern and Central European farmers of the 1700s and 1800s. As the country expanded westward during the mid-1800s, migrant workers began arriving from China, Japan, and other Asian countries. And the turbulent twentieth century brought an even greater variety of immigrants to Canada, from the Caribbean, Africa, India, and Southeast Asia.

So while English- and French-Canadians are the largest ethnic groups in the country today, neither group alone represents a majority of the population. A large and vibrant multicultural mix makes up the rest, particularly in Canada's major cities. Toronto, Vancouver, and Montreal alone are home to people from over 200 ethnic groups!

Less obvious but equally important in the evolution of Canadian immigration has been hope. The promise of a better life lured Europeans and

Americans seeking cheap (sometimes even free) farmland. Thousands of Scots and Irish arrived to escape grinding poverty and starvation. Others came for freedom, to escape religious and political persecution. Canada has long been a haven to the world's dispossessed and disenfranchised—Dutch and German farmers cast out for their religious beliefs, black slaves fleeing the United States, and political refugees of despotic regimes in Europe, Africa, Asia, and South America.

The two forces of diversity and hope, so central to Canada's past, also shaped the modern era of Canadian immigration. Following the Second World War, Canada drew heavily on these influences to forge trailblazing immigration initiatives.

The catalyst for change was the adoption of the Canadian Bill of Rights in 1960. Recognizing its growing diversity and Canadians' changing attitudes towards racism, the government passed a federal statute barring discrimination on the grounds of race, national origin, color, religion, or sex. Effectively rejecting the discriminatory elements in Canadian immigration policy, the Bill of Rights forced the introduction of a new policy in 1962. The focus of immigration abruptly switched from national origin to the individual's potential contribution to Canadian society. The door to Canada was now open to every corner of the world.

Welcoming those seeking new hopes in a new land has also been a feature of Canadian immigration in the modern era. The focus on economic immigration has increased along with Canada's steadily growing economy, but political immigration has also been encouraged. Since 1945, Canada has admitted tens of thousands of displaced persons, including Jewish Holocaust survivors, victims of Soviet crackdowns in Hungary and Czechoslovakia, and refugees from political upheaval in Uganda, Chile, and Vietnam.

Prior to 1978, however, these political refugees were admitted as an exception to normal immigration procedures. That year, Canada revamped its refugee policy with a new Immigration Act that explicitly affirmed Canada's commitment to the resettlement of refugees from oppression. Today, the admission of refugees remains a central part of

Canadian immigration law and regulations.

Amendments to economic and political immigration policy have continued, refining further the bold steps taken during the modern era. Together, these initiatives have turned Canada into one of the world's few truly multicultural states.

Unlike the process of assimilation into a "melting pot" of cultures, immigrants to Canada are more likely to retain their cultural identity, beliefs, and practices. This is the source of some of Canada's greatest strengths as a society. And as a truly multicultural nation, diversity is not seen as a threat to Canadian identity. Quite the contrary—diversity is Canadian identity.

1 "WE FELT DEATH UPON US"

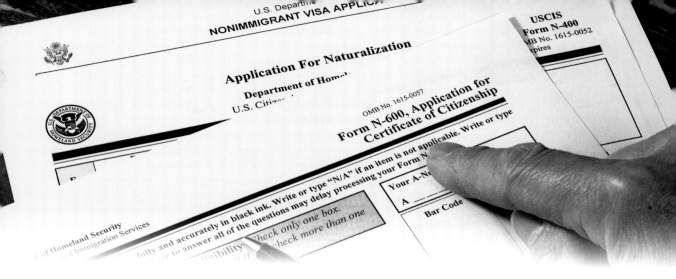

For residents of Daraa, a city of about 95,000 located in southern Syria, simply leaving the house had become a nerve-racking ordeal. Syria was in the midst of a savage civil war that pitted government forces loyal to dictator Bashar al-Assad against an array of groups fighting to overthrow him.

Daraa had played a key role in igniting the conflict. In March 2011, police arrested 15 young boys for spray-painting an anti-regime slogan on buildings in Daraa. In response, demonstrators gathered in the city to demand the release of the boys, and of all Syria's political prisoners. Security forces opened fire on the demonstrators, killing several. Protests quickly spread to other Syrian cities. The protesters called on Assad to step down.

As the unrest continued, Assad branded his opponents terrorists, and the regime cracked down with increasing brutality. Security forces killed hundreds of people at protests across the country. Civilians, joined by defectors from the Syrian army, struck back, attacking the security forces. By the summer of 2011, army defectors had formed a rebel group called the Free Syrian Army. Soon other groups, including Islamic extremist organizations, had joined the fight to overthrow Assad. A full-fledged civil war was under way.

◀ A crowd of Syrian refugees demonstrates against the regime of Bashar al-Assad while in a camp in neighboring Turkey. The Syrian Civil War that began in 2011 has created a refugee crisis, with millions of people fleeing the violence in the country.

Two years after the initial protests in Daraa, the government had yet to pacify the city. Each day, scores of people—many of them noncombatants—lost their lives in the fighting between government troops and rebels. Some were cut down in exchanges of gunfire between the two sides. Others were blown apart by mortar shells or bombs. Government forces often seized people from the streets and tortured and murdered them for suspected disloyalty to the regime. On the other hand, rebel groups were also known to offer young men they encountered the choice between joining them or being shot. The safest thing to do—though it was by no means a guarantee against sudden and random death—was to stay indoors and out of sight as much as possible.

Faez al Sharaa knew the risks of leaving his home. But he had a wife to provide for, so each day during the workweek he made a perilous walk through the streets of Daraa to his job at a health care company. One morning in late March 2013, Sharaa and three other men were stopped on the street by a squad of government troops. The soldiers accused the men of being terrorists and leveled their weapons. "We felt death upon us," Sharaa recalled, "and we accepted it."

Before the soldiers executed the captives, however, an old woman rushed into the street. She pleaded with the soldiers to release the men. They weren't terrorists, she insisted. They were her son, her nephew, and two neighbors. It was a lie—Sharaa

 Words to Understand in This Chapter

asylum—protection given by a country to people who have come as refugees from another country.

internally displaced person—a person who has been forced to move from one place to another within a country, because of persecution, war, or other factors.

non-refoulement—the principle that a government cannot force people to go back to a country or region where their lives or human rights will be endangered.

repatriate—to send someone back to a country of origin.

According to the UN High Commissioner for Refugees, by April 2016 more than 4.6 million Syrians had fled the country as refugees. Another 6 million were internally displaced within Syria.

had never seen the old woman before—but the soldiers were convinced. They let the men go.

Shaken by his brush with death, and convinced that he'd almost certainly be killed if he remained in Syria, Faez al Sharaa decided that he and his wife, Shaza, must get out of the country as soon as possible. That night, he contacted a group of local smugglers and arranged for a car ride to the border with Jordan. The smugglers would be making the eight-mile (13-kilometer) trip the following morning, regardless of whether Faez and Shaza al Sharaa showed up.

The Sharaas couldn't be picked up at their home—government checkpoints had effectively cordoned off their section of Daraa. Instead, the young couple picked their way through war-torn neighborhoods to meet their ride. At one point, a missile smashed into a nearby building. Had the building not absorbed the blast, Faez al Sharaa believes, he and his wife would have been killed. But after a harrowing 90-minute trek, the couple managed to reach the smugglers' car, and they were soon whisked to the border, where they successfully crossed over into Jordan.

In Search of Safety

Faez and Shaza al Sharaa were among an estimated 16.7 million refugees worldwide in 2013, according to the United Nations High Commissioner for Refugees (UNHCR). In simple terms, a refugee is someone who flees his or her country to escape armed conflict or persecution.

Every refugee's story is unique, of course. But fear, desperation, and hardship are common themes. Most refugees also feel a profound sense of dislocation and uncertainty; being a refugee typically involves months or even years of provisional living arrangements, as the Sharaas discovered.

After crossing into Jordan, the Sharaas were bused a short distance to Zataari, a teeming refugee camp set up in the desert by the Jordanian government and UNHCR, the United Nations' lead agency for the protection and support of refugees. Though Zataari offered safety, life was difficult in the sprawling camp of tents and makeshift buildings.

Shaza had relatives in Amman, Jordan's capital city, who offered to take the couple in temporarily. The Sharaas accepted the offer. They registered with UNHCR. That was the first step in a process that, the Sharaas hoped, would culminate with their resettlement in another country.

UNHCR officials did background checks and conducted an in-depth interview with the couple. Months passed. Shaza gave birth to the couple's first child, a girl. Faez did what he could to make money. He wasn't authorized to work in Jordan, but he got a low-paying job for which he was paid under the table. Though fortunate to be living in the home of relatives in Amman rather than in a tent in Zataari, the Shaaras were anxious to be resettled. Many Jordanians didn't bother to conceal their hostility. By 2014 more than 600,000 Syrian refugees had flooded into

Jordan—a country with fewer than 7 million people—and their presence put a severe strain on Jordan's limited resources and underdeveloped infrastructure.

The responsibility for determining whether a person seeking asylum should, in fact, be granted refugee status generally falls on the government of the country in which the asylum application is made. But UNHCR often assists by registering asylum seekers—gathering identifying information, detailing the reasons for the asylum claim, and recording other pertinent details. And when a government can't or won't process asylum applications, UNHCR may do so; it has the authority to make refugee-status decisions on its own.

To be certified as refugees, people must have a justified fear that their life or freedom would be threatened in the country they left. Those who leave their homeland for better economic opportunities—regardless of how poor they might be—don't qualify as refugees, and they may legally be sent home.

Once a person has been recognized as a refugee, however, that person has certain rights under international law. For example, refugees have the right to move freely within the country that has granted them asylum, the right to access that country's court system, the right to housing, the right to practice their religion freely, the right to work, and the right to education. Unfortunately, however, not every government lives up to its legal obligations with respect to the treatment of refugees.

Under normal circumstances, the determination of who does or doesn't qualify as a refugee is made on a case-by-case basis, after one or more asylum interviews (either by officials from the host country or UNHCR). Sometimes, however, the sheer number of people who flee across a border—for example, during a war—makes conducting individual asylum interviews impossible. In such cases, entire groups are often presumed to be legitimate refugees.

Refugee camps are supposed to be short-term measures for dealing with a crisis—although sometimes refugees do end up spending years in such camps. UNHCR pursues three durable,

أهلاً وسهلاً بكم
في كندا
WELCOME TO CANADA

A family of Canadian Muslims holds signs at Toronto's Pearson International Airport, welcoming the first Syrian refugees accepted to resettle in the country, December 2015.

or long-term, solutions for refugees. The first is repatriation—sending refugees back to their home country—after the threat to refugees' safety or freedom has been removed (for example, after a conflict has ended). If conditions in the refugees' home country remain dangerous for an extended period, however, a second option is integration into the asylum-granting society. The third, and least common, durable solution is relocation of refugees to a third country. UNHCR considers that a last option, appropriate only when refugees continue to be in danger in the asylum-granting country or the asylum-granting country cannot meet refugees' needs.

In such cases, UNHCR refers candidates for relocation to countries that resettle refugees within their borders. As of 2015, there were only 28 "resettlement countries." Historically, the United States has resettled more refugees, by far, than any other country. Canada, too, has been a leading resettlement country.

Other major resettlement countries include Australia and the Scandinavian nations.

Once a resettlement country has received the UNHCR's referral form for a resettlement candidate, immigration officials from that country evaluate the refugee's case. Procedures vary, but most resettlement countries conduct their own in-person interviews; often they also conduct their own background checks. A refugee accepted for resettlement is granted legal permanent resident status, including the eventual opportunity to become a citizen of his or her adopted country.

Resettlement Issues

Faez and Shaza Sharaa were interviewed again in preparation for what they believed would be their resettlement in Sweden. But that Scandinavian country, a nation of under 10 million, was overwhelmed by asylum requests from Syrians, as well as Iraqis and Afghanis. Facing a backlash from its citizens, the Swedish government decided to suspend its acceptance of any new refugees.

The Sharaas went through another round of interviews. They were informed they'd be headed to Sweden's eastern neighbor, Finland. But that arrangement also failed to materialize.

Finally, the family was accepted by the United States. On February 18, 2015—nearly two years after they'd fled Daraa, Syria—Faez and Shaza al Sharaa, with their young daughter in tow, landed in Dallas, Texas. With help from the International Rescue Committee, the family was placed in an apartment. The IRC, headquartered in New York City, is a nongovernmental organization that, among its other humanitarian work, aids in refugee resettlement. With help from an IRC caseworker, Faez got a job. Shaza delivered the couple's second child, another girl, who was an American citizen by birth.

There was other good news: the United States had accepted a half dozen of Faez's relatives from Syria. They, too, would be resettled in Dallas. For the Sharaa family, the future was looking bright.

But then, in late 2015, an unforeseen development darkened Faez al Sharaa's outlook—and that of Syrian refugees generally. Amid fears of terrorism, some American politicians began calling for a halt to the resettlement of Syrian refugees in the United States. Texas governor Greg Abbott was among 31 governors who said they'd block Syrian refugees from entering their state. "I'm very worried about my family," Faez confessed. Refugee advocates worried that the United States, a longtime leader in resettling refugees, was closing its doors to those most in need.

History of the Refugee

Throughout history, wars, persecution, and other crises have forced people to flee to other countries. Before the 20th century, many governments welcomed refugees from other countries. They saw these people as a means of improving their economies, or as new additions to the workforce and the army, so refugees typically did not face many restrictions. In the early years of the 20th century, however, attitudes in many quarters started to change. Governments began to view the unrestricted movement of refugees as a threat to their stability.

World War I (1914–18) caused the breakup of two empires: the Ottoman Empire and the Austro-Hungarian Empire. The latter had been notably multiethnic, and in the wake of its disintegration a handful of new nation-states were created. Ethnic tensions in these new countries produced many refugees.

However, it was the situation in Russia that prompted the international community to mount an organized effort to deal with the issue of refugees. In 1917, in the midst of World War I, a revolution overthrew Russia's monarchy. In the chaotic aftermath, a civil war broke out. It pitted the communist Bolsheviks (also known as the Reds) against the anti-communist Mensheviks (Whites). Eventually, the Bolsheviks gained the upper hand and, in 1922, established the communist Union of Soviet Socialist Republics. The civil war displaced more than a million people, most of them supporters of the Mensheviks. Existing international organizations such as the Red Cross lacked the resources to help the vast numbers of Russian refugees. In 1921, a newly formed organization for international security called the League of Nations established the Office of the High Commissioner for Refugees. The person who took this position was expected to give assistance to the Russian refugees and, if possible, to help repatriate them (send them back to their original country).

Leading up to the UN Refugee Convention

The first appointed High Commissioner for Refugees was Fridtjof Nansen, who remained in office until his death in 1930. Nansen immediately began looking for ways to help refugees, especially those in eastern Europe. During the 1920s, he provided travel documents not only to Russians but also to Armenian, Assyrian, and Turkish refugees. The documents made it easier for refugees to move legally from one place to another. Following the 1933 League of Nations Convention Relating to the International Status of Refugees, which guaranteed basic rights to refugees, displaced people now had a better chance to remain in the countries to which they had fled. Most refugees wanted to return to their original country—and most countries preferred to send them home—though this was often not a viable option.

During the 1930s, refugees fled the Nazi regime in Germany and Austria. Others escaped repressive governments in Italy and Spain. Many countries resisted taking in these refugees. In some

 Fridtjof Nansen

The first High Commissioner for Refugees appointed by the League of Nations, Fridtjof Nansen, was a former Arctic explorer. He completed the first-ever crossing of Greenland, which he achieved on skis with five other traveling companions. The first travel documents issued by the High Commissioner were known as "Nansen passports." For his service to refugees, Nansen received the Nobel Peace Prize in 1922.

countries, that was because of barriers to immigration by members of certain ethnic groups. Immigration by Italians to the United States, for example, was severely restricted under the Immigration Act of 1924. But economic considerations also played a major role. In the 1930s, industrialized nations suffered a severe and long-lasting economic downturn known as the Great Depression. With unemployment high and government resources strained, there was little appetite to admit large numbers of refugees. The U.S. State Department directed its consular officials overseas to refrain from issuing visas to anyone who might conceivably become a "public charge," including refugees. Canadian officials, too, sought to limit immigration for economic reasons.

During World War II (1939–45), the refugee problem worsened dramatically. Many Jews in Europe could not escape persecution and, later, death, because of immigration restrictions around the world, including those in Canada and the United States.

After being released from the Buchenwald concentration camp in Germany, 1945, Jewish refugee children depart for Palestine, where many European Jewish refugees resettled after World War II ended. Many other victims of the Nazi regime relocated to the United States and Canada.

Palestinian Arabs in a refugee camp set up by the United Nations in 1948. The Palestinians were fleeing a conflict between the newly formed State of Israel and its Arab neighbors.

World War II left millions of Europeans homeless. To address this crisis, the United States spearheaded the creation of the International Refugee Organization (IRO) in 1946. The IRO was an agency of the United Nations (UN), which was formed in 1945 to replace the League of Nations. The IRO's constitution guaranteed assistance to specially designated groups of refugees. Victims of the Nazi regime and orphans under the age of 16 were among those the IRO focused on repatriating or resettling. After the war, the organization helped some European and Asian refugees go back to their own countries, though most of them had to resettle in other countries. The United States accepted over 30 percent of the more than one million people resettled by the IRO.

The IRO was designed to be temporary; it was terminated in 1952. During the period of the IRO's service, the UN recognized the need for a more permanent agency to help the world's refugees. The 1948 Universal Declaration of Human Rights, drawn up by the UN Commission on Human Rights, included an article that stated, "Everyone has the right to seek and to enjoy in other countries asylum from persecution." In 1950, the United Nations High Commissioner for Refugees was established. UNHCR was designated as a non-partisan organization, headed by a leader also called the High Commissioner. Its first major mission was to help those who were made refugees by World War II. In July 1951, at a conference in Geneva, Switzerland, 26 nations adopted the Convention Relating to the Status of Refugees, a document that became the legal framework for UNHCR.

The Convention was much more detailed than any previous agreements relating to the classification and treatment of refugees. It defined a refugee as follows:

> [Any person who] . . . owing to well-founded fear of being persecuted for reasons of race, religion, nationality, membership of a particular social group or political opinion, is outside the country of his nationality and is unable or, owing to such fear, is unwilling to avail himself of the protection of that country; or who, not having a nationality and being outside the country of his former habitual residence . . . is unable or, owing to such fear, is unwilling to return to it.

The Convention also introduced the principle of *non-refoulement*, which committed governments not to turn refugees back to a home territory where their lives would be endangered or where they would be persecuted. This important principle has been part of refugee law ever since the 1951 Convention, although its application has not always been clear. The Convention did not specifically offer protection for internally displaced persons (IDPs).

After the 1951 Refugee Convention

Although the Refugee Convention was an essential step forward in the protection of refugees, it had many limitations. For instance, only those who had become refugees "as a result of events occurring before 1 January 1951" were considered "Convention Refugees." In addition, states that signed the

Convention were able to interpret the "events" clause to cover only events in Europe--and most states did just that. As a result, the Convention ended up applying primarily to European refugees.

Originally, the states that signed the Geneva Convention Relating to the Status of Refugees believed that major assistance to refugees would be required only for a few years, after which the European refugee problems stemming from World War II and its aftermath would be resolved. But during the 15 years that followed the Convention, major refugee crises arose elsewhere, especially in Africa. UNHCR was often able to provide humanitarian aid, but the specifications of the 1951 Convention were much too narrow to be applied directly to all refugee situations. Leaders in many countries realized that the Convention had to be extended so as to help a greater number of people.

In 1967, the UN passed the Protocol Relating to the Status of Refugees. It expanded the scope of the Convention on the Status of Refugees by removing the time and geographical limits. By the

Meal time at a refugee camp in Doroi, Mozambique. Over 15,000 refugees from Southern Rhodesia (Zimbabwe) were housed in this camp when the photo was taken in 1977.

end of the 1990s, over 130 states had accepted the Protocol, which includes the provisions of the Convention. The Protocol was not the final international agreement on the status of refugees, as the situations facing refugees have since changed frequently.

Refugee crises have continued to develop around the world for all kinds of reasons. Each refugee crisis has presented its own challenges, and since documents such as the 1951 Convention and the 1967 Protocol cannot apply to all situations, governments and organizations in different parts of the world have responded by drawing up agreements that fit local circumstances.

One such agreement was the Convention Governing the Specific Aspects of Refugee Problems in Africa, adopted by the Organization of African Unity (OAU) in 1969. One important distinction in this convention was that people could now become refugees as a result of disturbances or conflicts caused by "external aggression, occupation, [or] foreign domination." Another regional agreement was the 1984 Cartagena Declaration, made in response to the refugee crisis of the 1980s in Central America. Refugees had emerged in that region because of civil wars in Nicaragua, El Salvador, and Guatemala. Representatives from Mexico and Panama had adopted the declaration, which stated

 ## Resettling African Refugees

Until recently, North America has not been a major destination for African refugees. Most of them had gone to refugee camps in other parts of Africa, or to other parts of the Western world, such as Europe. In the last few years, though, many African refugees have been resettled in the United States and Canada. In 1998, the United States only resettled about 7,000 African refugees. In the year 2000, the number had increased to 18,000 refugees from 25 different African countries. In 2002, the United States agreed to take a segment of the 12,000 Somali Bantus, members of an ethnic minority group who had been refugees since the early 1990s. However, in that year only 2,566 refugees from Africa actually were admitted to America in 2002. Most of the African refugees who have resettled in the United States come from Ethiopia, Liberia, Somalia, and Sudan.

that people could claim refugee status as a result of "circumstances which have seriously disturbed public order." These and other new agreements made the 1951 Convention and the 1967 Protocol more inclusive to refugees, opening up possibilities to help victims in different parts of the world.

Although the Convention and the Protocol have greatly affected refugees around the world, there remain many countries that have never adopted these agreements. And even the countries that have adopted the Convention and the Protocol have applied them in very different ways. It's not surprising, then, that governments sometimes find themselves at odds over what to do about a particular group of refugees.

 Text-Dependent Questions

1. Where is Daraa?
2. What does UNHCR stand for?
3. Which country historically has resettled the most refugees?

 Research Project

Investigate the circumstances that led to the creation of Convention Governing the Specific Aspects of Refugee Problems in Africa. Present your findings in a one-page report.

2 REFUGEE POLICY THROUGH THE YEARS

The United States and Canada were founded by immigrants. Except for native peoples, whose ancestors have been in North America for thousands of years, no one in the United States or Canada can trace the history of their family on the continent back for more than five centuries. And most families have been in North America for a much shorter period than that.

American and Canadian attitudes toward immigrants, and toward refugees specifically, have fluctuated over time. During some periods, the United States and Canada have been less than welcoming to newcomers. In the main, however, the two countries have been havens for the world's refugees.

"As long as there are refugees," President Dwight D. Eisenhower declared in 1959, "we cannot ignore them." Though he considered it a moral imperative to aid those who had been displaced by persecution or conflict, Eisenhower also understood that the United States benefited from the contributions of the refugees it accepted. "Today," he said, "they are citizens; many of them own their own homes; some of them own their own businesses; their children are in our schools; and they, as families, are making a full contribution to our national life."

◀ Korean refugees use every possible means of transport on their journey south, December 1950. Refugees who resettle in the United States and Canada join the millions of immigrants who arrive looking for personal freedoms they might not have had in their own countries.

The United States has accepted more refugees for resettlement than all other resettlement countries combined. Canada, too, has been a leading country for refugee resettlement. In 1986, Canada received UNHCR's Nansen Refugee Award for its welcoming policies toward refugees—the first (and, as of 2016, the only) time the prestigious honor has gone to a country as a whole. (Eleanor Roosevelt, the former U.S. first lady, won the inaugural Nansen Refugee Award in 1954.) In the 1990s, Canada accepted more refugees in relation to its general population than any other country.

With their large resettlement programs and their stable and prosperous societies, the United States and Canada are beacons of hope to a great many refugees. In 2002, a Somali refugee awaiting resettlement in the United States said: "Going to America is a dream. It is the choice between the fire and paradise." UNHCR has said that Canada's refugee program is "in many ways a model of fairness and due process." That's not to suggest that the American and Canadian refugee programs don't have critics, both domestic and international. Some say that the two countries should accept more refugees (and, in the case of United States, should give more generous benefits to those it does admit). But some American and Canadian citizens believe their government already accepts too many refugees, or at least too many whose values might conflict with the values of the larger society. This concern has been expressed most often with regard to refugees from Muslim countries.

As neighbors and allies, the United States and Canada have

 Words to Understand in This Chapter

allegiance—loyalty to a government, leader, or cause.

asylee—a person who receives refugee status, meeting the legal definition of an individual who has a well-founded fear of persecution.

Holocaust—the mass killing of Jews by Nazi Germany during World War II.

often taken similar approaches to the refugee problem. They have worked together, coordinating on such matters as the movement of refugees between the two countries. But they have also sometimes taken different approaches to refugees.

A Closer Look at Refugee Policy

Although the United States and Canada have both done a great deal to help refugees—since World War II, in particular—there have been occasions when their commitment fell short. The most famous of these incidents occurred in 1939.

In May 1939, more than 900 German Jews boarded a passenger ship, the *St. Louis*, in Hamburg, Germany. It was a few months before the outbreak of World War II, but Germany's Nazi regime had already begun persecuting Jews. The Jewish refugees had obtained visas to visit Cuba, where the *St. Louis* was bound. From there, they hoped to make their way to the United States. But when the *St. Louis* arrived in Havana, Cuban authorities refused to let anyone disembark, and after the ship had been at anchor for a week, the passengers' visas were canceled. The Cuban government apparently wanted to avoid spurring a wave of Jewish refugees from Europe.

The *St. Louis* then headed for Florida. It passed close enough to Miami for passengers on deck to hear music coming from waterfront hotels and clubs. But U.S. authorities refused the vessel permission to dock, and the *St. Louis* was forced to return to Europe.

Fortunately, the passengers weren't returned to Germany. England, France, Belgium, and the Netherlands agreed to accept Jewish refugees from the ship. However, after Nazi armies overran the latter three countries during World War II, more than 250 of the people who'd set sail on the *St. Louis* were killed in the Holocaust.

Eight years after the *St. Louis* incident, Congress passed the Displaced Persons Act, the first U.S. law to deal specifically with refugees. It allowed Europeans uprooted by World War II to become permanent residents of the United States. In the 1950s and 1960s, Congress passed more acts to help refugees. Under the 1952 McCarran-Walter Act, the U.S. attorney general had the authority to let unlimited numbers of refugees enter the country temporarily. The 1953 Refugee Relief Act and the 1957 Refugee-Escapee Act gave refugee status to people escaping Middle Eastern countries and communist countries in Eastern Europe. In 1968, the United States accepted the 1967 Protocol to the 1951 United Nations Convention Relating to the Status of Refugees, an important development because the United States had originally not accepted the Refugee Convention.

Between 1975 and 1980, large numbers of refugees arrived in the United States from Vietnam and other Southeast Asian countries. American policies—particularly U.S. involvement in the Vietnam War—were at least partly responsible for creating the flood of refugees, and many Americans believed the United States had a moral obligation to help them. Many legislators and other government officials saw the need to improve U.S. refugee policy generally. In 1979 Joseph Califano, the secretary of the Department of Health and Human Services, pleaded for the admission of more refugees into the country. He stated: "By our choice on this issue, we reveal to the world—and more importantly to ourselves—whether we truly live by our ideals or simply carve them on our monuments." A year later, Congress passed the Refugee Act of 1980.

Previously, the United States had scrambled to respond as each new refugee crisis arose. The Refugee Act paved the way for a more orderly process: each year, based on a review of conditions in troubled regions of the world, the president sets (with congressional approval) the maximum number of refugees the country will admit. The Refugee Act established a resettlement program—including sponsorships, job placement services, and language training—designed to ensure that refugees became self-sufficient as quickly as possible after entering the United States. The new law also recognized asylees, people who apply for refugee status *after* they've already arrived in the country, either legally or illegally.

A Pakastani man passes through the Islamabad International Airport after being deported from the United States in July 2003. A group of Muslims was deported after September 11, 2001, for being in the country illegally.

Since the act's passage, a variety of American organizations have worked to help refuges in the world at large. In 1989 a national branch of UNHCR, USA for UNHCR, was established. This volunteer organization raises money and awareness for the UN agency.

After September 11

After the terrorist attacks of September 2001, refugees were among those most severely affected. For two months, the U.S. government suspended its refugee resettlement program, and as a result 20,000 refugees suddenly could not enter the country. One of the results of the program's suspension was that fewer refugees were admitted to the United States in 2002 than in any year since 1987, according to the World Refugee Survey, issued by the U.S. Committee for Refugees. The United States admitted only 27,075 refugees in 2002, less than half the number of

North America's First Refugees

The arrival of refugees is not a new development in American and Canadian history. Starting in the 1600s, and over the next three centuries, many of the people who arrived on the shores of North America were fleeing religious or political persecution; others were fleeing famine or extreme poverty. During this time, people also moved across the border between the United States and Canada, in both directions.

Some of the earliest arrivals in the future United States were Puritans. This Christian group disagreed with the practices of the Church of England. Because of their criticism of the Church, they became victims of prejudice and discrimination in England, and could not freely practice their faith. Some of the Puritans left for Holland, a move that did not improve their situation a great deal. In 1620, a group of Puritans sailed from Holland to Massachusetts aboard the *Mayflower*. Other Puritans arrived in New England over the next few decades.

In 1754 a war erupted between France and Great Britain, along with their respective North American colonies, over control of the interior of the continent. British colonists would call the conflict the French and Indian War. The people living in what are today the Canadian Maritime provinces—New Brunswick, Nova Scotia, and Prince Edward Island—had been under British rule since 1710. But these people, known as Acadians, were the descendants of French colonists, and the British suspected their loyalties lay with France. In 1755, the British tried to compel the Acadians to swear an oath of allegiance to the British crown. When they refused, the British declared them "non-citizens" and expelled more than 10,000 from their homes and their land. The British general in charge of removing the Acadians described the operation as "a Scene of Woe and Diestress." British soldiers destroyed the Acadians' farms and houses so that there would be nowhere for them to go if they escaped. Some of the Acadians went to the French colony in Louisiana, while others went to New England. Eventually, a number of the exiles returned home.

During the Revolutionary War (1775–83), American colonists fought for independence from Britain. But up to 500,000 people living in the American colonies continued to support British rule. These Loyalists faced discrimination because of their politics. Many of them lost their houses and properties. About 50,000 Loyalists left the United States for Canada, the largest wave departing after the American victory. Many Loyalists were originally from England, but there were also Scottish, Dutch, and German Loyalists. In Canada, they settled in areas such as Nova Scotia and Ontario. A Loyalist memorial in Nova Scotia bears the inscription: "They sacrificed everything save honour."

Before the abolition of slavery, there were millions of black slaves living in the United States, a large number of whom refused to accept a lifetime of slavery. Between 1786 and the 1865, black refugees fled to freedom in Canada by means of the Underground Railroad, a network of houses and routes run by people willing to help the slaves. Many escaped slaves did not make it. However, about 40,000 slaves reached Canada through the Underground Railroad. After the end of the Civil War (1861–65), about half of these refugees returned to the United States.

refugees admitted in any of the previous 10 years.

An additional reason that fewer refugees were admitted in 2002 was that they faced new procedures after the September 11 attacks. A series of security enhancements were added to help prevent fraud or the entry of those who could be a national security threat to the United States. The new security procedures and others added later—including name checks against U.S. and international law enforcement and terrorism databases, extensive verification of family relationships, and the use of biometric data such as fingerprints and iris scans—have significantly slowed the processing of refugees.

Understanding U.S. Refugee and Asylee Law

Refugees and asylees both must have a "well-founded fear of persecution," but under U.S. law there is a difference between the two groups. Generally speaking, a refugee is someone who is interviewed outside the United States and an asylee is interviewed inside the country.

While the term *refugee* is often used for both groups of people, this distinction is important. An asylum seeker—someone who wants to become an asylee—may come to the United States on a tourist visa, or even use fake documents. He or she will then request asylum either affirmatively, by going to a government immigration office, or will ask for asylum as a defense against being deported from the country. If an asylum officer does not approve that claim, the asylum seeker can go before an immigration judge for a final decision. If the person is in custody and seeking to avoid being deported, an immigration judge, rather than an asylum officer, will hear the case first. Under its international commitments, neither the United States nor Canada will deport an individual who will be tortured in their home country; however, some individuals who have committed serious criminal offenses or who represent a national security threat may be denied asylum.

The Bureau of Population, Refugees, and Migration (PRM) in the U.S. Department of State takes a leading role on U.S.

refugee policy in partnership with the U.S. Citizenship and Immigration Services (USCIS) and the Office of Refugee Resettlement in the Department of Health and Human Services (HHS). In addition to managing funds appropriated by Congress to relieve humanitarian and refugee crises overseas, a primary mission of PRM is to set policy guidelines for the refugee admissions program. These guidelines govern who should be eligible for interviews, what the priorities are for those interviews, and how refugees who are admitted should be resettled. (American refugee organizations, often religiously affiliated, try to coordinate with PRM to establish resettlement guidelines.)

Every year, PRM, in coordination with other federal agencies, prepares a report with recommendations for how many individuals from each region of the world should be admitted in the next fiscal year. Ultimately, however, it is the president, in consultation with Congress, who decides on the worldwide refugee "ceiling" for the year. Each year the secretary of state or another cabinet-level official meets with the leaders of the House and Senate judiciary committees to discuss the refugee admission numbers. While there is usually some give-and-take, the administration's initial proposal has traditionally been the same as the final number that the president usually announces prior to the beginning of the next fiscal year.

Interviews are conducted overseas not by the State Department but by refugee adjudicators, or interviewers, who are part of the USCIS. These adjudicators must assess the credibility of the person sitting before them by weighing his or her answers to questions and examining documents he or she may present. Voluntary agencies, usually U.S.-based refugee organizations under contract to the government, may assist refugees in preparing their cases. UNHCR will generally act as a "gatekeeper" and refer several thousand individuals a year as prospects for resettlement in the United States.

Since there are so many refugees to select for interviews, the State Department has established a priority system. Priority 1 (P-1) status is given to refugees whose need for resettlement is very

UN officials interview a Sudanese refugee in a camp in neighboring Chad.

high. Priority 2 (P-2) is for "specific groups (within certain nationalities)" of special concern. Other priority levels are based on family relationship with a U.S. citizen or lawful permanent resident. Such a family relationship is an interview priority, but it is not sufficient for gaining refugee status—the individual still must show he or she has a legitimate reason for fearing persecution. Although many people receive refugee status every year, PRM still receives criticism for setting interview criteria that are too restrictive and thus prevent legitimate refugees from even having the opportunity to present their cases.

Those who are granted refugee status can work in the United States. After living in the country for one year, they can apply to stay permanently, and after five years, they can usually apply for U.S. citizenship. Refugees can receive medical help and other types of special assistance right away, while other immigrants have to wait five years to become eligible for these benefits. Asylees are also authorized to work after being granted asylum. However, USCIS's Asylum Division often has a large backlog of cases. In mid-2015, for example, some Asylum Division offices still hadn't processed the applications of affirmative asylum seekers from 2013. This places a burden on the applicants, who aren't legally permitted to work until their cases have been resolved.

Canadian Refugee Policy

After World War II, Canada resettled many refugees from countries such as Hungary and Czechoslovakia. Although the Canadian government most eagerly accepted young, skilled refugees, it also sought to help many simply on the grounds that their lives were in danger. Still, refugees did not have many basic rights in Canada until 1969, when the Canadian government accepted the 1951 UN Refugee Convention and its 1967 Protocol.

During the 1970s, changes in refugee policy allowed for Canada to accept refugees at a growing rate. Refugees were placed in a specially designated class that was exempt from Canada's immigration points system. The pivotal 1976 Immigration Act—implemented in 1978—established the Refugee Status Advisory Committee (RSAC), which was respon-

 The Melting Pot of America

A conventional metaphor for American society is the "melting pot." The image symbolizes America's inclusiveness, as well as the assimilation expected of different cultures to help form a national culture. The "melting pot" expression originally comes from the title of a 1908 play by Israel Zangwill, a British writer and son of Russian immigrants. In the play, a Russian-Jewish composer named David Quixano wants to write a symphony about his new country, the United States. He sees America as "a divinely appointed crucible in which all the ethnic division of mankind will . . . become fused into one group, signifying the brotherhood of man."

sible for looking at refugee claims in detail. This act recognized that refugees did not always fit the standard classification and that new refugee categories should be created whenever necessary.

The Canadian government took a controversial step in 2000 when it eliminated the Right of Landing Fee (ROLF) for refugees. In existence since 1995, the ROLF helps cover the costs of programs for people who have just arrived in Canada. When the decision was announced, Elinor Caplan, the Minister of Citizenship and Immigration, said: "Refugees have already faced enormous difficulties and stresses. By eliminating this fee we help them to get on with their lives and to integrate successfully into Canadian society." Some people felt that this decision was unfair, since other immigrants continued to pay the ROLF.

Canada's partnership with the United States has greatly influenced its refugee policy. In October 2002, the two governments signed the Safe Third Country Agreement, which required that asylum seekers make their request for protection in the first safe country—defined under Canadian law as a country that respects human rights and offers a high degree of protection to asylum seekers—in which they arrive. As of 2016, the United States was the only country Canada had designated as a safe third country. Canada recognizes a few exceptions to the "first safe country" rule, including asylum seekers with family members who are Canadian citizens, and unaccompanied minors.

In the past, many asylum seekers had arrived in the United States but then continued on to the Canadian border to take advantage of Canada's services to newcomers. Some estimates say that 75 percent of the people seeking asylum in Canada first arrived in the United States. Under the Safe Third Country Agreement, however, Canada generally doesn't accept asylum seekers who have crossed the border from the United States.

Defenders of the Safe Third Country Agreement argue that once people have reached a safe country, they should remain there. This, it's maintained, helps ensure that governments share the responsibility for refugee claims, and that one or a few countries aren't unduly burdened. However, some officials and refugee advocates asserted that the Safe Third Country Agreement would increase illegal crossings of the U.S.-Canada border. As a gesture of compromise, Canada agreed that it would resettle up to 200 refugees a year who were officially referred by the United States. The U.S. government also adopted a policy of allowing those asylum seekers with relatives in the United States to apply for asylum there.

The refugee admittance process in Canada is similar to the American process. Canadian immigration officials go to refugee camps and other places, interview potential refugees, and offer refugee status to selected individuals. There are three basic ways refugees from abroad can be resettled in Canada. First, under the Government-Assisted Refugees Program, refugees are referred by UNHCR or an NGO. Once accepted for resettlement, they're supported entirely for up to a year by the Canadian government or by the government of a province. Second, under the Private Sponsorship of Refugees Program, refugees are referred for resettlement by private sponsoring groups in Canada. Such groups include churches, community organizations, and even small collections of concerned individuals. Groups of as few as five Canadian citizens or permanent residents are eligible to sponsor refugees. Privately sponsored refugees usually receive financial and social support from their sponsors for one year, though in some cases sponsorships may extend for up to three years. Third, refugees may be resettled in Canada through a hybrid process known as the Blended Visa Office–Referred (BVOR) Program. The BVOR Program essentially creates a three-way partnership between UNHCR, which refers the refugees; the Canadian government, which provides up to six months of financial support; and private sponsors, which provide an additional six months of financial support as well as a year of social support. All resettled refugees are granted permanent resident status as soon as they arrive in Canada.

Canada, it's widely acknowledged, stands as an international leader in the practice of refugee protection. Adrienne Clarkson, who came to Canada as a refugee during World War II and went on to serve as Canada's governor-general from 1999 to 2005, summed up her country's welcoming stance toward displaced people. "Canada has a great track record for giving," Clarkson said, "and I would like us to continue to be committed to it forever. . . . I think we have to do even more than our share, because we have so much more."

 Text-Dependent Questions

1. Where was the *St. Louis* headed? What did its passengers hope would happen when the ship arrived?
2. Name the first U.S. law specifically intended to deal with refugees.
3. Why did refugee admissions to the United States drop dramatically in 2002?

 Research Project

UNHCR maintains a list of past Nansen Refugee Award winners at the following website:
http://www.unhcr.org/pages/49c3646c467-page1.html
   Choose one winner and do some in-depth research. Write a one-page essay about the recipient's life and work.

3 REFUGEES FROM SOUTHEAST ASIA

Vietnam, Laos, and Cambodia are Southeast Asian countries located on a large peninsula south of China and east of India. Together, the three countries are often called Indochina, though that designation properly refers to the entire peninsula and also includes Thailand, Myanmar (formerly called Burma), and part of Malaysia.

Beginning in 1975 and continuing for two decades thereafter, waves of refugees—some 3 million people in all—fled Vietnam, Laos, and Cambodia. Tens of thousands died in their bid to escape persecution. About a half million others eventually returned to their home countries. But more than 2 million were resettled abroad. The United States took in about 1.3 million, and Canada admitted close to 200,000. The refugee crisis was touched off by war and political upheaval.

The French in Indochina

During the latter half of the 19th century, France gained control, in stages, of the territory that now makes up Vietnam, Cambodia, and Laos. It established the colony of Indochine, or French Indochina.

◀ Refugees from Cambodia, Vietnam, and Laos are processed at the Lumbhini Transit Centre in Bangkok, Thailand, 1979. About 2,000 people from this camp would be admitted to the United States. Since 1975, the United States and Canada have accepted more than 1.3 million refugees from Southeast Asia.

In 1940, during World War II, Japanese forces invaded and quickly conquered French Indochina. Japan permitted French administrators to continue governing the colony (albeit in a manner that aided Japan's war effort) until March 1945, when the Japanese killed or imprisoned the administrators and took direct control of Indochina.

From 1943 on, Japanese troops in the northern part of Vietnam had been harassed and attacked by a Vietnamese guerrilla group organized in China. The group was called the Viet Minh, after its leader, Ho Chi Minh. The United States was also fighting Japan, and the Viet Minh—who were largely composed of communists— provided information about Japanese troop movements to American intelligence officers. The group also helped rescue downed American pilots.

On September 2, 1945, when Japan officially surrendered and World War II came to an end, Ho Chi Minh proclaimed the independence of Vietnam. He announced the founding of the Democratic Republic of Vietnam. France, however, had other ideas. By year's end, French troops were landing in Vietnam to reestablish control of the Indochina colony.

Ho Chi Minh pleaded with the United States to prevent France from recolonizing Vietnam, citing the principles of equal rights and self-determination for all peoples enshrined in the charter of the newly founded United Nations. "I . . . most earnestly appeal to you personally and to the American people

 Words to Understand in This Chapter

communism—a political and economic system that advocates the elimination of private property, promotes the common ownership of goods, and typically insists that the Communist Party has sole authority to govern.

communist—a follower of communism; relating to or characteristic of communism.

guerrilla—a member of a usually small group of soldiers who don't belong to a regular army and who fight as an independent unit; relating to the irregular tactics used by such a group.

to interfere urgently in support of our independence," he wrote in a February 1946 telegram to President Harry S. Truman. The appeal fell on deaf ears: For a variety of reasons, American policy makers had decided not to oppose French actions in Vietnam.

In late 1946, fighting erupted between French forces and Vietnamese seeking independence, led by the Viet Minh. France attempted to placate its foes by setting up the semi-autonomous Associated State of Vietnam in 1949. The State of Vietnam, headed by a former emperor named Bao Dai, claimed authority over all of Vietnam. But the Viet Minh insisted that Bao Dai was a puppet of the French, and the fighting continued.

By 1954 the Vietnamese had decisively defeated the French. An international conference in Geneva that year produced a set of agreements known as the Geneva Accords. The accords specified that Vietnam, Laos, and Cambodia would gain full independence from France. Laos and Cambodia were to hold national elections in 1955. Vietnam would be divided temporarily at the 17th parallel of latitude. The area north of that line would be controlled by the communist Democratic Republic of Vietnam, which was dominated by the Viet Minh. South of the partition line, a successor government to the State of Vietnam would be established. Vietnamese civilians would have 300 days to relocate north or south of the 17th parallel if they so desired. Elections would be held in 1956 to select a national government for a unified Vietnam.

The Vietnam War

In 1955 the United States helped an anti-communist named Ngo Dinh Diem come to power in the newly created Republic of Vietnam—or South Vietnam, as it was commonly called. Diem soon announced that he'd block the 1956 elections the Geneva Accords had called for to reunify Vietnam. If those elections were held, Diem would almost certainly have lost to Ho Chi Minh.

Diem's decision to prevent the Vietnamese people from voting for their government had the full support of the United

States. American foreign policy had become focused on one overarching goal: containing the spread of communism worldwide. And if a communist government were allowed to gain power in Vietnam, U.S. policy makers feared, Vietnam's neighbors would also fall to communism—like a row of dominoes after the first is tipped over, in the memorable image of President Dwight D. Eisenhower.

Thus, what the Geneva Accords envisioned as a brief, provisional partition of Vietnam led to the creation of two separate countries: North Vietnam, with its capital in Hanoi, and South Vietnam, with its capital in Saigon. That situation, however, wouldn't last.

Communists remained in South Vietnam, and Diem launched a series of brutal campaigns to root them out. By 1957 communist guerrilla fighters known as the Viet Cong had begun retaliating by assassinating South Vietnamese government officials in the countryside. By the end of the decade, the Viet Cong were engaging units of South Vietnam's army, and the government of North Vietnam had decided to overthrow the South Vietnamese regime with military force.

As the conflict intensified, U.S. involvement gradually grew. During the latter half of the 1950s, the United States had, in addition to supplying weapons and equipment, kept about 800 military advisers in South Vietnam to assist its army. By 1962 that number had increased to about 9,000; by 1963 some 16,000 U.S. military advisers were in South Vietnam. Still, the South Vietnamese armed forces—whose leadership earned a well-deserved reputation for corruption and incompetence—were unable to gain the upper hand.

By late 1963 Diem—who was himself notoriously corrupt, brutal, and deeply unpopular—had lost the confidence of his military. In November of that year, a group of South Vietnamese generals (with the tacit approval of U.S. officials) ousted and killed Diem. But corruption and incompetence continued to plague the South Vietnamese government and armed forces.

South Vietnam now seemed especially vulnerable, and North

Smoke rises from firebombed buildings in Saigon after the Viet Cong launched the Tet Offensive, a major battle of the Vietnam War, January 1968. The war, which ended in 1975, produced hundreds of thousands of refugees.

Vietnamese leaders decided the time was right for a decisive blow. In 1964 North Vietnamese regular army units began crossing into South Vietnam to join Viet Cong guerrillas in the fight against the South Vietnamese army. On August 2, however, North Vietnamese patrol boats skirmished with a U.S. Navy destroyer in the Gulf of Tonkin, off the coast of North Vietnam. There were no American casualties. U.S. warships reported another North Vietnamese attack in the Gulf of Tonkin two days later. Though historians have concluded that no such attack occurred, President Lyndon B. Johnson ordered airstrikes against North Vietnam and asked Congress to pass a resolution approving his use of "all necessary measures to repel any armed attack against the forces of the United States and to prevent any further aggression." Congress complied, and the Johnson administration used the Tonkin Gulf Resolution to escalate U.S. involvement in Vietnam. By 1965 more than 180,000 American combat troops were fighting in Vietnam, and troop levels steadily increased in the years that followed, peaking at more than half a million in 1968.

U.S. casualties mounted as well, and the American public became more and more bitterly divided over the war. Richard M. Nixon, elected president in 1968, pursued a strategy of "Vietnamization." The goal was to build up South Vietnam's armed forces so that U.S. troops could gradually be withdrawn.

To compensate for the drawdown in American ground forces, the Nixon administration ordered a massive—and secret—bombing campaign. It targeted areas inside Laos and Cambodia where North Vietnamese or Viet Cong forces had sanctuary, in addition to the so-called Ho Chi Minh Trail, the network of roads and trails by which North Vietnam moved supplies and troops into South Vietnam. In 1970 Nixon also authorized U.S. ground troops to cross into Cambodia and attack North Vietnamese forces there.

In January 1973 representatives of North Vietnam, the Viet Cong, South Vietnam, and the United States signed "An Agreement Ending the War and Restoring Peace in Vietnam," better known as the Paris Peace Accords. The agreement imposed a cease-fire and required the United States to withdraw all its remaining military personnel (about 25,000 men in all) within 60 days. North and South Vietnam committed to a peaceful, negotiated process for reunifying the country.

But the Paris Peace Accords didn't hold. Both sides committed small-scale violations of the cease-fire, and by 1974 the war had resumed in earnest, though without U.S. participation. South Vietnamese resistance collapsed in the face of a major communist offensive launched in early 1975. Fearing for their safety, about half a million South Vietnamese fled toward Saigon ahead of the advancing North Vietnamese and Viet Cong forces. But the fall of the capital city—and with it, South Vietnam—was now inevitable. On April 30, 1975, with the communists on the outskirts of Saigon, South Vietnam's newly installed president, Duong Van Minh, ordered his forces to surrender. More than two decades after the Geneva Accords had partitioned Vietnam, the country was finally unified under a communist government.

The human costs of the Vietnam War were staggering. All told, it's estimated that at least 1.3 million people had lost their lives (including some 58,000 Americans), and millions more were wounded and maimed. Related conflicts in Laos and Cambodia had claimed the lives of several hundred thousand others.

But for many civilians, the end of the fighting only marked the start of a new ordeal. In the coming years, hundreds of thousands of Indochinese refugees would flee their countries.

The First Wave of Indochinese Refugees

Even before the fall of Saigon, the United States had taken steps to help address an anticipated refugee crisis, which President Gerald Ford called "a tragedy unbelievable in its ramifications." On April 4, Operation Babylift was launched. This program brought 2,000 Vietnamese orphans to new homes in the United States.

In the weeks leading up to the communist victory, the United States sought to evacuate South Vietnamese who were closely associated with the American presence in Vietnam, as these people were considered at great risk for retaliation. In all, the United States transported about 140,000 refugees by ship or by airplane from South Vietnam.

In the early morning hours of April 29, 1975, North Vietnamese forces shelled Saigon's airport, making its runways impassable—and scuttling plans to evacuate thousands of people by airplane later that day. Thus began "Operation Frequent Wind," a frantic, last-ditch effort to evacuate remaining Americans (including staff of the U.S. Embassy) as well as desperate South Vietnamese by helicopter. About 90 American helicopter pilots flew nonstop, shuttling more than 7,000 people from points in Saigon to U.S. warships offshore in less than 24 hours. It was the largest helicopter evacuation in history.

The Vietnamese refugees were brought to the United States.

They were placed temporarily in refugee camps on military bases, set up through a program called Operation New Life.

Vietnamese refugees who did not receive help directly from the United States fled to other Southeast Asian countries, such as Thailand, where many stayed on American military bases. Eventually, most of these refugees ended up going through Operation New Life and arriving in the United States. Voluntary agencies (VOLAGs) worked to find sponsors for the refugees and to help them resettle in the United States. These organizations tried to distribute the refugees across the country, hoping they would become integrated into American society and not become isolated within their own ethnic communities.

Refugee Programs and Organizations

The American response to the arrival of some 140,000 Vietnamese refugees was mixed. In 1975, the U.S. economy was

Vietnamese refugees on board a police boat, southwest of Hong Kong, 1989. More than two decades after the Vietnam War, hundreds of Indochinese people are still escaping repressive governments. Although it is not as active today as it was in the 1970s, the Orderly Departure Program still helps resettle these refugees in the United States.

weak. Many people felt that the arrival of the refugees would only make the economic situation worse, and that the U.S. government should concentrate on helping its own people. Others wanted to do all they could for the new arrivals. Special programs helped the refugees to learn English and to receive social and medical care. The VOLAGs placed the Vietnamese children in school and helped the adults to find work.

Most of the refugees ended up staying in the United States, although a few thousand went to other countries. In general, they did not have too many problems fitting in with American society. A lot of the people in this first wave of refugees came from middle-class backgrounds. More than a quarter of them had a college education. Within two years of their arrival, almost 95 percent of them had found jobs; within seven years, there was a higher employment rate among the first wave of Vietnamese refugees than among the U.S. population in general.

In 1976, a year after the end of the Vietnam War, Canada accepted about 6,500 Vietnamese refugees. Vietnamese communities already existed in Canada before the 1970s, most of them in the French-Canadian province of Quebec because so many Vietnamese immigrants already spoke French as a result of France's occupation. Sixty-five percent of the first-wave refugees resettled in Quebec, where many relatives of the refugees had already settled.

By the end of 1975, the American camps for Vietnamese refugees were closing. Many people thought the crisis was over. Lionel Rosenblatt of the Interagency Task Force, one of the U.S. government organizations that had helped with the refugee resettlement program, said: "[At the end of 1975], by and large we thought the evacuation would be it. There wasn't ever a vision that this would be an ongoing refugee program."

But developments in Indochina would spur massive new movements of refugees. In Laos, a communist revolutionary group known as the Pathet Lao overthrew, with considerable support from North Vietnam, the U.S.-backed Royal Lao Government in 1975. Once in power, the Pathet Lao mercilessly attacked opponents such as the Hmong ethnic group, who had been closely allied with the United States.

In Cambodia, another communist group supported by North Vietnam ousted a U.S.-backed government in 1975. The group, known as the Khmer Rouge, instituted a staggering reign of terror in the pursuit of what it regarded as a pure form of communism. Between 1975 and 1979, when Vietnam invaded Cambodia and overthrew the Khmer Rouge, the regime systematically murdered at least 1.7 million of its people.

In Vietnam, too, severe repression followed the communist takeover. About a million former officials in the South Vietnamese government, army officers, church leaders, and others were sent to "reeducation camps," which were actually forced-labor prison camps. Sentences typically ranged from 3 to 10 years, though some people were kept longer. As many as 165,000 died from exhaustion, malnutrition, disease, or beatings.

The Boat People and Other Indochinese Refugees

In the reunified, communist Vietnam—which was officially renamed the Socialist Republic of Vietnam—reeducation camps ranked among the harshest measures by which the government took retribution against residents of the former South Vietnam. But reeducation camps weren't the only form of punishment. For example, the government also seized the property of and evicted from their homes up to a million people, mostly in southern cities. Northerners, often Communist Party officials or soldiers, moved into the confiscated homes, while the former owners were forcibly resettled in desolate mountainous areas euphemistically called "New Economic Zones." This guaranteed they would be desperately poor.

In the face of government oppression, some Vietnamese sought to escape to other Southeast Asian countries by sea. For several years, their numbers amounted to only a few thousand. In the fall of 1978, however, the trickle of boat-borne refugees

South Vietnamese refugees aboard a sailboat; they left the country after North Vietnamese forces captured the city of Saigon, April 1975.

turned into a wave. Some gained passage aboard freighters or commercial fishing boats. Others, however, crammed into small, rickety boats never designed for the open seas. They headed for Malaysia, Indonesia, Thailand, the Philippines, Singapore, Hong Kong, or even faraway Australia.

The voyages of these refugees, dubbed the "boat people," were fraught with peril. Tens of thousands drowned when their boats sank. Untold numbers of others were preyed on by pirates. Still others died of exposure or starvation.

By the end of 1978, more than 60,000 boat people were in refugee camps throughout Southeast Asia—and the numbers fleeing Vietnam were increasing steadily every month. Adding to that were flows of Laotian and Cambodian refugees, who made their way over-land into Thailand.

The situation entered a dire new phase after Indonesia, Malaysia, and Thailand began stopping boat people from land-ing on their shores. Their coast guards often towed vessels back out to sea. Singapore refused entry to any refugees who didn't have a third-country guarantee of resettlement within three months.

The United States accepted modest numbers of boat people for resettlement. So did Canada, which in November 1978 agreed to accept 600 of 2,500 refugees aboard a ship that had arrived in Hong Kong harbor. But given the scope of the prob-lem, the response seemed woefully inadequate. Many Americans and Canadians called on their governments to do more to help the boat people.

The Indochinese refugee crisis reached a tipping point in mid-1979. In June, some 54,000 boat people arrived along the shores of Southeast Asian countries. And those countries already had about 350,000 Indochinese refugees in all. During the first half of 1979, three new Indochinese refugees had arrived for every refugee who'd left for a resettlement country. In late June, the members of the Association of Southeast Asian Nations (ASEAN)—which then included Indonesia, Malaysia, the Philippines, Singapore, and Thailand—declared that they'd "reached the limit of their endurance" and wouldn't accept any new refugee arrivals.

In July, under the auspices of the UN, an international conference was convened in Geneva to address the Indochinese refugee crisis. The conference resulted in important commitments. The ASEAN countries agreed to accept more refugees. In return, countries such as the United States, Canada, France, and

These Vietnamese refugees are waiting in a detention camp in Cambodia, 1972. When that country fell under the control of the communist Khmer Rouge government, many of them would attempt to migrate to the United States.

Australia promised to dramatically step up the pace of resettlement. For its part, Vietnam pledged to try to stop its citizens from leaving the country without authorization. One component of that pledge was the Orderly Departure Program (ODP), devised by UNHCR. Under the terms of the ODP, Vietnam would allow citizens to emigrate for the purpose of family reunion or for other humanitarian reasons.

The agreements obtained at the July 1979 conference brought the Indochinese refugee crisis under control. The flow of boat people began to decline almost immediately. During the latter half of 1979, approximately 25,000 refugees were resettled per month, up from about 9,000 per month during the first half of the year. By July 1982, more than 20 countries had collectively resettled nearly 624,000 Indochinese refugees since the conference in Geneva. The United States resettled the lion's share of those refugees.

In the late 1980s, the number of people leaving Vietnam without authorization and requesting asylum in neighboring countries again spiked. Analysts suggested that many of these people weren't refugees but were instead economic migrants, and that the surge in migration coincided with the Vietnamese government's relaxation of restrictions on travel within the country—which made it easier for migrants to get close to a land border or coast, thereby facilitating their departure.

Neither Vietnam's Southeast Asian neighbors nor the world's refugee resettlement countries had much appetite for dealing with another mass migration of Vietnamese. In 1989, at another international conference held in Geneva, a program for dealing with the situation was hammered out. Known as the Comprehensive Plan of Action (CPA), it eliminated the presumption that Vietnamese requesting asylum deserved refugee status. Asylum claims would be heard individually, and Vietnamese judged not to have a well-founded fear of persecution would be promptly repatriated. At the same time, the Vietnamese government pledged to allow more of its citizens the opportunity to immigrate legally. A U.S.-Vietnam agreement expanded the ODP to include former reeducation camp detainees and political prisoners, as well as children conceived during the Vietnam War by American fathers and Vietnamese mothers. In all, more than half a million Vietnamese would come to the United States before the year 2000 under the ODP. By then the United States had accepted about a half million other Vietnamese refugees, a quarter million Laotian refugees, and more than 150,000 Cambodian refugees.

In the past couple decades, the governments of Vietnam, Laos, and Cambodia have been fairly stable, and the United States has admitted relatively small numbers of people from those countries as refugees. During the 10-year period 2004–2013, for example, fewer than 16,000 Laotian refugees, and fewer than 12,000 Vietnamese refugees, were resettled in the United States. Only about 100 Cambodian refugees came to the United States during that period.

Indochinese refugees settled across the country. However, the largest concentrations are in California, Texas, and the state of Washington.

The Indochinese in Canada

In the decades since the Vietnam War, Canada has opened its doors to more than 200,000 Indochinese refugees. The vast majority—about 8 in 10—are Vietnamese. And of that group, about 60,000 were boat people resettled between July 1979 and January 1981.

Four provinces are home to the vast majority of Canada's Indochinese people: Alberta, British Columbia, Ontario, and Quebec. Vietnamese Canadians are concentrated in four major metropolitan areas: Toronto, Ontario; Montreal, Quebec; Calgary, Alberta; and Vancouver, British Columbia. Significant portions of the smaller Laotian Canadian population also can be found in Ottawa, Ontario.

The years of conflict in Vietnam and other parts of Indochina left behind a tragic legacy. Millions had to flee their homes, triggering one of the largest refugee crises in history. Before the

Indochinese refugee crisis, the United States and Canada never had to deal with a refugee movement on such a large scale. Eventually, both countries rose to the challenge. Through new laws, government programs, and the generosity of individuals and private organizations, nearly 2 million Indochinese refugees have been able to rebuild their lives in North America.

 Text-Dependent Questions

1. Which European country colonized Vietnam, Laos, and Cambodia?
2. What did the U.S. Congress pass the Tonkin Gulf Resolution? What was its significance?
3. What does ASEAN stand for?

 Research Project

Use the Internet to see if you can find how many people of Vietnamese, Laotian, or Cambodian extraction live in your state or province.

4 CRISIS IN THE CARIBBEAN

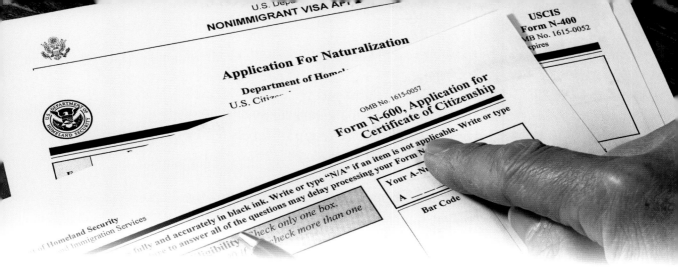

The large Caribbean island of Cuba lies less than 100 miles (161 km) south of the tip of Florida. Just a short distance to the east of Cuba, across the Windward Passage, is Haiti. This country occupies the western side of another large island, Hispaniola, whose eastern side is occupied by the Dominican Republic.

For many people, the word *Caribbean* brings to mind beautiful beaches and a restful way of life. However, Cuba and Haiti have suffered from political repression and desperate economic problems for decades. Over the years, hundreds of thousands of people from these two countries have sought asylum in the United States. But U.S. policy toward would-be Cuban and Haitian refugees has differed dramatically, creating controversy.

Troubled Relations

Cuba was a Spanish colony for four centuries. During the second half of the 1800s, though, Cubans took up arms and tried several times to win their independence. In 1898, amid one such fight for Cuban independence, the United States declared war on Spain. The Spanish-American War ended quickly, and with Spain decisively defeated. As a result, Spain lost Cuba, which became independent in 1902 (though until the 1930s the United

◄Cuban president Fidel Castro delivers a speech shortly after leading a coup to oust dictator Fulgencio Batista, January 1959. Castro instituted a communist regime as president, and many Cuban refugees who have since emerged have received asylum as a result of the anti-communist policies of the United States and Canada.

States claimed a right to intervene in Cuban affairs under certain circumstances).

In 1952, a former president and army officer named Fulgencio Batista seized control of Cuba's government. Batista became a ruthless and corrupt dictator. A group of rebels led by a lawyer named Fidel Castro formed to overthrow the Batista regime. In January 1959, they succeeded.

Large numbers of Batista supporters fled, many for the United States, in the face of the rebel takeover. But Batista had been unpopular, and Castro promised an honest, democratic government. Most Cubans were optimistic about their country's future—at least at first.

At the highest levels of the U.S. government, there was concern about Castro's ideological leanings. American policy makers wondered whether Cuba's new leader was a communist. During an April 1959 trip to Washington, D.C., Castro offered a public reassurance about his political philosophy. "I know you are worried . . . first of all if we are communist," he said at a news conference. "And of course . . . I have said very clearly that we are not communist."

Yet Castro soon began dismissing moderate members of his government and replacing them with avowed communists. And in early 1960, Cuba signed a major trade agreement with the Soviet Union, the main communist adversary of the United States. Meanwhile, businesses in Cuba—including American-owned companies—were nationalized. Cubans who criticized the government were imprisoned, and independent newspapers

Words to Understand in This Chapter

embargo—a government prohibition on trade with another country.

exiles—people who've left their nation (voluntarily or otherwise) for political reasons.

interdict—to intercept and prevent the movement of people or goods.

nationalize—to transfer (a business or industry) from private ownership to government control.

were closed down.

In October 1960, President Dwight D. Eisenhower imposed a trade embargo on Cuba, banning all U.S. exports to the island except for food and medicine (the embargo would later be expanded to include U.S. imports from Cuba). In January 1961, the United States formally cut diplomatic relations with Cuba.

But the U.S. government was planning more drastic measures. The Central Intelligence Agency had armed and was training a group of Cuban exiles to invade Cuba and overthrow Castro. In April 1961, the exiles landed at a place called the Bay of Pigs, but Cuban forces quickly routed them.

Within a month of the Bay of Pigs invasion, Castro publicly declared that Cuba would follow the path of communism and was allied with the Soviet Union. That alliance nearly led to disaster when, in October 1962, the United States discovered that Soviet nuclear missiles were being set up in Cuba. President John F. Kennedy demanded that the missiles be removed, and a tense, 13-day standoff ensued, during which the United States and the Soviet Union appeared to be on the brink of a nuclear war. Finally, the Soviets agreed to remove the missiles, and the crisis was defused.

Relations between Cuba and the United States, however, could hardly have been worse. The two countries would remain bitter foes for decades.

Golden Exiles and Refugees

Soon after Fidel Castro came to power in 1959, some of Cuba's best-educated and most-prosperous citizens began leaving the island and moving to the United States. They were doctors, lawyers, engineers, businesspeople, and other highly trained professionals. Castro's suppression of dissent and his communist policies, including the seizure of private businesses and of personal assets belonging to the wealthy, spurred many of these so-called Golden Exiles to leave Cuba.

At first, the exiles were able to take money and valuable possessions with them when they boarded commercial airliners and headed for the United States. But the government soon began taking everything of value from the people it allowed to leave the country. Still, upper- and middle-class Cubans continued to depart in large numbers (few Cubans of modest means could scrape together enough money to purchase an expensive exit visa, which the government required for anyone wishing to leave the island). By 1962, more than 200,000 Golden Exiles had moved to the United States. Most assumed their stay would be fairly brief. They believed Castro would soon be overthrown, whereupon they'd be able to return to Cuba and resume their former lives. As the years passed, though, it became more and more clear that the Castro regime was entrenched.

From the outset, the U.S. government welcomed Cubans as political refugees. Once they arrived in the United States, Cubans received assistance through the Nine-Point Program, which provided access to health and job services, schooling, and other essentials. This program fell under the Migration and Refugee Assistance Act of 1962. In Miami, Florida, the Cuban Refugee Emergency Center assisted with job placement and resettlement. Cubans called the center *El refugio*—"the Refuge" in Spanish.

In the wake of the Cuban Missile Crisis, all commercial flights between Cuba and the United States were eliminated. With no easy way to get to the United States, the northward flow of Cubans declined dramatically. But it didn't entirely disappear. Some Cubans tried to get to the United States by first flying to a third country. Others who couldn't afford an exit visa attempted a much more perilous journey. They sneaked away from Cuban shores aboard boats and tried to cross the Straits of Florida. Some perished at sea. Others were caught and imprisoned for leaving the country without permission. But between 1962 and 1965, an estimated 30,000 Cuban refugees—many of them in small, overcrowded boats—successfully sailed from Cuba to Florida.

In September 1965, Castro made a surprise announcement: the following month, his government would allow citizens who wished to immigrate to the United States to depart from the port of Camarioca. Cuban Americans would be permitted to bring boats to the port to pick up relatives or friends. U.S. officials agreed to the arrangement but tried to ensure the boatlift followed an orderly process. It didn't. By November, when Castro abruptly closed Camarioca's port, the boatlift had degenerated

 ## Refugees from Central America

Like so many other areas of the world, Central America has suffered from refugee crises. During the 1980s and 1990s, countries such as El Salvador, Guatemala, Honduras, and Nicaragua experienced civil war, human rights abuses, and extreme poverty. By 1990, it was estimated that there were 2 million Central American displaced people in the world. Many of these people were internally displaced; others had moved to a different Central American country, Mexico, or the United States.

Despite the refugee crises in these countries, most Central American refugees did not enter the United States legally. There was no "refugee processing" in the region (U.S. officials interviewing potential refugees in Central America). Therefore, the primary option for Central Americans fleeing oppressive governments and violence in the 1970s and 1980s was to come to the United States and seek asylum. In 1985, a group of religious and human rights organizations collaborated on behalf of Guatemalan and Salvadoran asylum applicants and filed the *ABC v. Meese* lawsuit. The suit claimed that the U.S. government was unfairly dismissing legitimate claims of persecution, in part due to U.S. support for their governments. The lawsuit was finally settled in 1991 in favor of the asylum seekers. Those who were denied asylum before were at least offered another interview to reassess their claims.

However, when Congress passed the Illegal Immigration Reform and Immigrant Responsibility Act (IIRAIRA) in 1996, it became harder for individuals who lived in the country illegally to avoid deportation. Provisions of the act adversely affected many Central Americans. In 1997, after the Central American immigrant issue received much public attention, Congress passed the Nicaraguan and Central American Relief Act (NACARA). The law lowered the standard that Salvadorans and Guatemalans—including those in the *ABC* class-action lawsuit—had to meet in order to remain in the country. In addition, NACARA made it even easier for Nicaraguans to stay in the United States: generally speaking, it gave those who arrived in the country before 1995 permanent residence or green cards. Many observers believed that Nicaraguans received preferential treatment as a result of their greater political influence among Republicans in Congress.

At certain times, Canada has allowed groups of Central Americans to enter the country. In 1983, Salvadorans made up over 40 percent of all people moving to Canada from Central and South America. With the help of the Canadian government and some churches, 296 political prisoners and their families entered Canada in the early 1980s. In 1984, a special initiative allowed some Guatemalans to come to Canada as refugees.

into chaos.

Cuba and the United States soon negotiated another means for Cubans to immigrate to the United States: "Freedom Flights." U.S.-chartered airliners would make twice-daily flights to Miami from Veradero, Cuba. The Cuban government placed many restrictions on who was eligible for the Freedom Flights, which began in December 1965. But by April 1973, when the program ended, some 250,000 Cubans had come to the United States on the Freedom Flights. Unlike the so-called Golden Exiles, few Cubans who arrived during this period were highly educated professionals. The majority had been employed as factory workers, agricultural laborers, or in similar blue-collar occupations.

After the discontinuation of the Freedom Flights, the number of Cuban arrivals in the United States declined. Over the next few years, some Cubans who wanted to immigrate to America first went to Spain. The U.S. government established programs that would bring them from Spain and reunite them with family members in the United States. In addition, as had occurred earlier, Cubans continued trying to cross the Florida Straits in small boats. The risks were great, but so was the potential reward of escaping Castro's regime and starting a new life in the United States. The U.S. Congress and President Lyndon B. Johnson had created extra incentives through a 1966 law, the Cuban Adjustment Act. It gave special status to Cubans under U.S. immigration law. Any Cuban who arrived in the United States or was picked up at sea by the U.S. Coast Guard—regardless of whether the person had proper documents—would automatically be granted asylum and become eligible for permanent resident status in the United States in two years (later reduced to one year). Undocumented migrants from other countries, by contrast, were subject to arrest and deportation; those who requested asylum had to prove their individual claims at a hearing.

During the latter part of the 1970s, relations between the Cuban exiles and Fidel Castro improved somewhat, and Castro began allowing Cuban exiles to visit their homeland. He also ordered the release of 3,000 political prisoners. President Jimmy Carter in 1977 began a push to improve U.S. relations with Cuba. Three years later, in 1980, no one was prepared for the events that would create the Cuban refugee crisis known as the Mariel boatlift.

The Mariel Boatlift

In April 1980, six Cubans in a bus rammed through the fence surrounding the grounds of the Peruvian embassy in Havana and requested asylum. Within a week, 10,000 other Cubans had flooded onto the embassy grounds and asked for asylum. Peru did not want to take them as political refugees, however, and so the United States agreed to accept them. Fidel Castro announced that he was lifting the restrictions on those who wanted to leave Cuba, but on the condition that the refugees go directly to the United States and no other country.

A boat full of Cuban refugees arrives in Key West, Florida, as part of the massive Mariel boatlift of 1980. More than 125,000 refugees were involved in the boatlift, which was prompted by President Castro's sudden decision to lift restrictions on emigration.

On April 21, thousands of Cubans living in Florida arrived in Cuba's Mariel Harbor in hired boats. Thus began the Mariel boatlift. President Jimmy Carter announced that the United States would welcome the refugees with "an open heart and open arms." Over the course of seven months, 125,000 Cubans had arrived by boat.

The Mariel boatlift operation became difficult to manage because the refugee group was not limited to friends and relatives of those already living in the United States. Following Castro's directive to get rid of Cuba's "antisocial elements," Cuban officials had opened a number of the country's jails and mental hospitals and put the inmates onto the Mariel boats. A U.S. House Appropriations Committee report found that approximately 10 percent of the Mariel Cubans may have possessed a mental illness or criminal background that would have made them ineligible to enter the United States under the law.

Eighth Street (Calle Ocho) is located in the heart of Miami's Little Havana neighborhood. The state of Florida is home to the largest population of Cuban Americans.

The American public was less supportive of this new wave of refugees than it had been of past arrivals on the shores of Florida. The U.S. economy at the time was weak, and many people felt that the sudden arrival of thousands of refugees would only make matters worse. Around the end of May, the government began to seize boats and impose fines. The Mariel boatlift came to an end.

Most of the Mariel refugees, who became known as "Marielitos," were able to stay in the United States, though in some cases their status of refugees remained uncertain for years. Some criminals were classified as "excludable aliens"—in the past, a term used to describe those who had not yet entered the country. The refugees who were criminals and had already entered the United States were detained indefinitely, although they had already served time for their crimes. Others were classified as "entrants, status pending."

The Marielitos faced unique challenges, some of which were posed by Cubans already resettled in America. Marielitos and the pre-Mariel refugees disagreed over many things. Siro del Castillo, former director of a refugee center in Miami, understood the source of the conflict: "The Marielitos demanded respect for having to endure the Castro regime. Meanwhile, the exiles [pre-Mariel refugees] were saying, 'We worked very hard to get what we have.'"

However, the Marielitos believed they had also endured much to become a part of American society, and they were ready to take advantage of their new opportunities. By 1985, most of them were able to become permanent residents. A few years later, they were able to start bringing family members over from Cuba. Like earlier generations of refugees, the Marielitos were eager to help new refugees from Cuba, even if they were not family members. During the 1980s, they had great success in assimilating into American society, enjoying the highest levels of employment of any immigrant group in Florida.

Cuban refugees continued to enter the United States with little difficulty until 1994, when the U.S. government had to confront major refugee crises involving thousands of Cubans and Haitians wishing to enter the country. These two crises were related in many ways, and so it is helpful to first become familiar with Haitian refugee history leading up to 1994.

The Haitian Refugees

Throughout most of its history, Haiti has been plagued by political instability, corruption, and violence. It's also impoverished—in fact, Haiti perennially ranks as the poorest nation in the Western Hemisphere.

Two of the country's most infamous leaders were a father and son: François Duvalier (known as Papa Doc), who ruled from 1957 to 1971, and Jean-Claude Duvalier (Baby Doc), who ruled from 1971 to 1986. The two dictators persecuted their critics and used a brutal private militia called the Tonton Macoutes to terrorize ordinary people into submission. They lived lavishly while the vast majority of Haitians were desperately poor.

Before 1970, a small number of Haitians, primarily consisting of political refugees, had come to live in the United States. But it was not until the early 1970s that Haitians began arriving in the United States in large numbers. Groups usually set out for Florida, traveling by boat across the same stretch of water as those Cuban refugees bound for the United States.

But the similarities between the plight of Cuban and Haitian refugees ended there. In 1981 the U.S. Coast Guard regularly began stopping Haitian boats and forcing them to turn back. Some boats near U.S. shores were towed back out to sea to ensure that the Haitians did not attempt entry again. Most of the Haitians who managed to reach Florida were denied asylum and deported. Some escaped detection and joined the Haitian community as undocumented immigrants.

The dramatic difference in the way Haitian and Cuban migrants were treated had much to do with the Cuban Adjustment Act. And that law had been passed, at least in part, because the United States was bitterly opposed to Cuba's communist government and American legislators wanted to spotlight the repressiveness of the regime. The Duvaliers were brutal dictators, but they weren't communists, and the United States maintained normal diplomatic relations with Haiti. Although many people in Haiti have suffered persecution, U.S. immigration officials have typically viewed Haitian refugees as individuals escaping poverty, not political oppression.

Since no law like the Cuban Adjustment Act existed for Haitians—or any other nationality—those who landed in the United States from Haiti had to demonstrate that they have a "well-founded fear of persecution." Economic deprivation, a generalized fear of violence, or dissatisfaction with the political regime is not sufficient under U.S. law to receive asylum.

The number of Haitian boat people coming to the United States increased in 1980, around the time of the Mariel boatlift. Human rights groups and others demanded that the Cubans and the Haitians be treated in the same way. Like many of the Cuban refugees, the Haitians were classified as "entrants, status pending," but unlike the Cubans, they still could not apply to stay permanently in the United States.

In 1981, the U.S. government made an agreement directly with the Haitian government. Haiti would take back people who were trying to leave and enter the United States illegally, and the U.S. Coast Guard would start to interdict, or stop from entering the country, all boats arriving from Haiti. Although the Coast Guard was only supposed to send back undocumented immigrants, not refugees, most Haitians attempting entry were turned back between 1981 and 1991.

After a popular uprising forced Jean-Claude Duvalier to flee Haiti in 1986, the country experienced considerable political instability. But in 1990 Haiti held elections that observers said were the freest and fairest in the nation's history. A Catholic priest named Jean-Bertrand Aristide won the presidency. Aristide served for less than eight months before he was ousted in a military coup. Violence in Haiti spiked. Soon another wave of Haitians tried to leave the country. Some went across the eastern border to the Dominican Republic, while others headed for the United States in boats.

Although U.S. officials continued to interdict Haitians who were on their way to the United States, they temporarily stopped returning them to Haiti and instead moved them to the military base at Guantánamo Bay, Cuba. There the Haitians went through a screening process to determine if they could apply for refugee status in the United States. Out of 34,000 Haitians taken to Guantánamo Bay during this period, 10,500 were able to go to the United States and apply for refugee status, although most of them were not admitted. Guantánamo Bay was called a "safe haven," but some human rights organizations argued that it was more like a prison than a place of shelter.

After six months, Guantánamo Bay was closed to the Haitians. Once again, the Coast Guard began sending refugee boats back, and the repatriation program continued until 1994, the year that the overwhelming numbers of Haitians and Cubans attempting to emigrate led to major refugee crises.

The Refugee Crises of 1994

Cuba began to experience serious economic problems in the early 1990s. The 1991 collapse of the Soviet Union, Cuba's communist ally, made matters worse for the country. An increasing number of Cubans tried to leave the country and go to the United States. In 1994, the situation became desperate. When Cuban officials tried to stop the refugees from leaving, they staged riots in protest. Even worse, some refugees hijacked ferries in an attempt to reach Florida. The Cuban government once again lifted restrictions on leaving the country, and much like the Mariel boatlift of 1980, Cubans started departing in large numbers. The U.S. Coast Guard picked up many of the 30,000 who fled, though dozens died at sea.

The U.S. government believed that it could not deal with such large numbers of people claiming refugee status. Most of the refugees were taken to Guantánamo Bay instead of Florida. In August 1994, President Bill Clinton's administration reached

These Haitian refugees were interdicted by the U.S. Coast Guard in November 1991. A new wave of refugees emerged that year after the overthrow of President Jean-Bertrand Aristide paved the way for another period of persecution and oppression.

an agreement with the Cuban government. The United States would no longer allow all Cubans to enter the country, and the Cuban authorities would try to restrict the mass departure of its citizens. The United States would hand out, at minimum, 20,000 entry permits every year, though these were only for those who were granted permission to emigrate by Castro's regime. The U.S. government began holding lotteries every few years to determine who would receive the 20,000 slots.

Haitian refugees saw their situation improve temporarily in

1994. In June, the U.S. government set up a refugee application center on board the USNS *Comfort*, a hospital ship. The U.S. Navy stationed the *Comfort* off the coast of Jamaica. Coast Guard officers took interdicted Haitian refugees on board the ship and processed their applications. Many of the Haitian refugees who went on board were granted refugee status.

Over the next few weeks, though, the *Comfort* could not cope with the waves of refugees fleeing Haiti. The United States responded by opening additional refugee application centers. Haitian soldiers destroyed boats in an attempt to stop people from leaving. During one incident at Baie du Mesle, on the southern coast of Haiti, soldiers fired on a boat carrying hundreds of refugees. When the panicked refugees tried to dodge the gunfire, dozens of them fell into the water and drowned.

And yet the flow of refugees continued to increase. Aristide, in exile in the United States while waiting to return to power, refused to urge Haitians against leaving. "It would be immoral to ask people whose very lives are at risk to stay in Haiti, a Haiti I am compelled to describe as a house on fire," he said.

Although the United States could not process such a large number of refugees, American officials also realized that they could not send the Haitians back to their country at this time. Once again, Guantánamo Bay was opened to the Haitians. From July until September 1994, 21,000 Haitians stayed at the naval base. In September, after the U.S. military threatened to invade Haiti if the regime did not relinquish its control, an accord was reached. When Aristide returned to power, most of the Haitians at Guantánamo Bay returned as well.

In the beginning of 1995, thousands of Cubans were still being held at Guantánamo Bay. In May, the U.S. government agreed to allow most of them to enter the country. But the era of easy migration for Cuban refugees was coming to an end. Over the next year, the United States and Cuba agreed that Cubans who wanted to enter the United States would have to go through legal programs for refugees and immigrants.

The United States developed the "wet foot, dry foot" policy

toward Cuban refugees. Simply put, those Cubans who made it to shore would be allowed to stay and those Cubans who were interdicted at sea and never made it to U.S. soil would be returned to Cuba after getting an opportunity to apply for refugee status.

In 1998, the U.S. Congress passed the Haitian Refugee Immigration Fairness Act. Under this new law, Haitians who had applied for asylum before 1996 were now able to apply for permanent residence. By the late 1990s, the number of undocumented Haitians trying to reach the United States by boat was relatively small, and most who did attempt the journey were interdicted by the Coast Guard and denied entry into the United States. The issue of Haitian refugees had begun to recede from the American public's consciousness when a 2002 incident sparked renewed controversy. In October of that year, a ship with more than 200 Haitian refugees on board ran aground off Key Biscayne, Miami, and as usual, the refugees were picked up and detained. Around the same time, a Cuban pilot loaded seven of his relatives onto a government-owned cargo plane and flew it to Key West's airport. The Cubans requested asylum, and immigration officials promptly released them to join relatives in Florida.

In a controversial policy decision first implemented in December 2001, in the wake of the September 11 terrorist attacks, the Bush administration started to detain almost all Haitians who made it to U.S. soil via boat. Attorney General John Ashcroft stated that the policy was necessary to prevent a mass migration and, in the spring of 2003, invoked national security to justify the continuing detention of the Haitians. This policy meant that rather than being let out on bond while their asylum claims were being decided, Haitian men and women would remain locked up for nine months or more in prison, albeit separated from criminals.

In recent years, relatively few Haitians have been granted asylum in the United States. From 2004 to 2013, according to the Office of Immigration statistics, the total was 11,430—an average of only 1,143 per year.

For Cubans, meanwhile, the door to automatic permanent resident status for "dry foot" refugees may be closing. In December 2014, President Barack Obama and Raúl Castro—Fidel Castro's brother and successor as leader of Cuba—announced plans to begin normalizing relations between their respective countries. In July 2015, full diplomatic relations were restored. Some American officials called for a reexamination of the preferential treatment of Cubans under the Cuban Adjustment Act. "The Cuban policy should be changed," Representative Henry Cuellar, a Texas Democrat, flatly declared in late 2015. "If we do that for them, why not do it for the Central Americans, the Mexicans, and for everyone else?"

Refugee Life in the United States

Today, a large number of Cubans and Haitians live in New York City. There are also sizeable Cuban communities in New Jersey and California. But Florida has by far the highest Cuban and Haitian populations in the United States. According to data from the U.S. Census Bureau, the Haitian American population totaled about 535,000 in 2010, with more than 45 percent living in Florida. Two-thirds of the nation's 2 million Cuban Americans live in Florida, and they're heavily concentrated in Miami–Dade County—which is home to more than 45 percent of all Cuban Americans. Miami's Little Havana neighborhood is a popular area for tourists, featuring Cuban restaurants, stores, and monuments dedicated to Cuban figures of the past and present. The headquarters of Alpha 66, a Cuban anti-Castro political group, is in Little Havana's Plaza de la Cubanidad. Little Haiti, though much less wealthy than Little Havana, also has colorful stores, especially those that sell Caribbean food and religious items.

Many Cubans are involved in U.S. politics, and have a clear influence on American policy regarding their home country. Cubans living in the United States come from a wide variety of social and educational backgrounds. Those who arrived before the Mariel boatlift were generally well educated. They have contributed greatly to helping the refugees who came during and after the Mariel boatlift.

Some Cubans are well established in the United States and would prefer not to leave under any circumstances. Others would choose to leave if Cuba transitioned to a democracy. Alex Cambert, a correspondent for the morning TV program *Good Morning America*, gave an account of his family's immigrant history. He said:

> My father came from Cuba for what he thought was a temporary stay, and is still hoping for the demise of Castro. I'm born here and know that my parents' struggle gave me the freedom to choose, even if that means rejecting the very things my parents adhere to.

The Haitian community in the United States has experienced more serious problems than the Cuban community has. In 2010, it was estimated that there were 125,000 undocumented Haitians living in the United States.

Haitian immigrants have worked hard to become productive members of American society. Some outspoken migrants have drawn attention to the differences in how the government has treated Cuban and Haitian refugees. All have faced the challenge of becoming American while still remaining Haitian.

 # Text-Dependent Questions

1. Who led the successful effort to overthrow Cuban dictator Fulgencio Batista in January 1959?
2. The flow of Cuban refugees entering the United States slowed abruptly in late 1962. Why?
3. Who were Papa Doc and Baby Doc?

 # Research Project

Create a timeline for Cuba or Haiti, beginning around 1900 and continuing to the present.

5 REFUGEES FROM THE MIDDLE EAST

There is no universal agreement on what constitutes the Middle East. But the region is commonly thought to include the Arab countries of North Africa, the lands of the eastern Mediterranean (Israel, the Palestinian territories, Jordan, Lebanon, and Syria), the Arabian Peninsula, Iraq, Iran, and Turkey.

The Middle East gave birth to some of the world's earliest civilizations, and to three of the world's major religions. Although Islam is dominant in the Middle East, the region is also the birthplace of the Jewish and Christian faiths. The Western world has always been interested in the Middle East; since the early 20th century, it has taken particular interest in its oil and other valuable natural resources.

For hundreds of years, the mixture of the Middle East's different religions, political systems, and cultures, accompanied by the intervention of foreign powers, have generated continual turmoil. Countries have been racked by war and religious persecution. Especially since the 1950s, the eyes of the world have turned again and again to this troubled region, where wars and oppressive governments have created millions of refugees.

◄ Iranian demonstrators march with a shrouded body in 1978; mourning ceremonies like this one were often accompanied by rioting and violence between Islamic rebels and the Iranian government. The Iranian Revolution ended with the ascension of the Ayatollah Khomeini in January 1979, who instituted an oppressive regime that produced hundreds of thousands of refugees.

The Iranian Refugee Crisis

In the early years of the 20th century, Persia—as Iran was formerly known—was one of the first Middle Eastern countries in which oil reserves were found. The discovery sparked the interest of many Western countries, which began to influence the region's politics and culture. In 1908, the Anglo-Persian Oil Company, a British firm, was established. It soon became one of the most important oil companies in the world.

Throughout its history, Persia had been ruled by absolute monarchs from a series of dynasties. In the first decade of the 20th century, however, a constitution was introduced to limit the powers of Persia's shahs, or kings.

In 1921 a military officer named Reza Khan seized power in a coup. Within five years, he compelled Persia's parliament to crown him as the new shah. In 1935 Reza Shah Pahlavi, as he called himself, changed the name of his country to Iran.

The shah's pro-Nazi leanings impelled British and Soviet forces to occupy oil-rich Iran in 1941, during World War II. Reza Shah Pahlavi was deposed and his son, Mohammad Reza Pahlavi, was placed on the throne.

After the war, the shah became embroiled in a power struggle with Iran's prime minister, Mohammad Mossadeq. Mossadeq championed the nationalization of Iran's petroleum industry, which was dominated by the Anglo-Iranian Oil Company (the new name of the British company founded in 1908). The shah opposed nationalization, but Mossadeq prevailed, and popular demonstrations against the shah's rule

 Words to Understand in This Chapter

ayatollah—a religious leader of the Shia branch of Islam.

cleric—a person who is a leader of a religion and who performs religious services.

depose—to remove from a throne or other high position.

Under the Ayatollah Ruhollah Khomeini (1900–1989), Iranians were subject to the worst forms of persecution. Many of his political opponents were executed before they could flee the country.

forced him into exile in 1953. That exile lasted all of one day. A coup orchestrated by the British intelligence service and the U.S. Central Intelligence Agency overthrew Mossadeq. After his return, the shah became much more ruthless in dealing with his opponents.

In the early 1960s, the shah undertook a campaign to modernize and Westernize Iran. He reorganized Iran's legal and educational systems along European lines. He promoted women's rights. He encouraged Iranians to wear Western-style clothing. These reforms weren't welcome in certain quarters of Iran, which was a highly conservative society. Many people thought the reforms went against the principles of Islam. The stage was set for what became known as the Islamic Revolution (1978–79).

In the early 1960s, a group of Muslim clerics opposed many of the current shah's liberal reforms. Their leader, the Ayatollah Khomeini, was sent into exile in Iraq. By 1978, many Iranians were unhappy with the shah's government, particularly its Western orientation, its brutal secret police, and the lavish spending of the royal family. Khomeini, who was living in Paris, insisted that the shah step down. Massive demonstrations against the shah took place. When the government tried to put them down violently, the demonstrations only grew. In January 1979, the shah left Iran, and Khomeini returned to take control. Soon a theocracy, the Islamic Republic of Iran, was established. At its head was Khomeini, who held the title of Supreme Leader.

Before the Islamic Revolution, many Iranians had left their country to study or to work in other countries. Most of them had planned to come back to Iran, though they were impeded by Khomeini's new intolerant regime. Khomeini declared that the other Middle Eastern countries were not truly Muslim, and that the Islamic Revolution should be extended to overthrow these countries' governments. Under the shah, Iran had been an ally of the United States. Now, Khomeini declared the United States as the "Great Satan." The Iranian hostage crisis, in which 52 Americans were held in captivity between November 1979 and January 1981, made relations between Iran and the United States even worse.

As it consolidated power, Khomeini's regime executed thousands of supporters of the shah, members of moderate and liberal political parties, and ordinary people the regime deemed immoral, such as homosexuals and adulterers.

People who belonged to religions other than Islam also became targets. They included Jews and members of the Baha'i religion, considered an Islamic heresy by the state. At the time of the Islamic Revolution, there were more than 300,000 Baha'is in Iran. Under the new regime, Baha'is had their property and jobs taken away; some lost their lives. Realizing that the group was facing a desperate situation, UNHCR announced that any Iranian Baha'i could claim refugee status. The Baha'is, along with other religious minorities, became one of the largest refugee groups to flee Iran.

Hundreds of thousands of Iranians left Iran after the revolution. Many of them remained in Turkey or Pakistan. By 1988, there may have been close to 2 million Iranian refugees in these

 The Iranian Hostage Crisis

The Iranian hostage crisis began on November 4, 1979. On that day, about 500 Iranian students, angry that the exiled shah had been allowed into the United States for medical treatment, seized the U.S. embassy in Tehran. Negotiations and a rescue mission to free the hostages failed. On January 20, 1981, the hostages were finally freed. The crisis had lasted for 444 days.

countries. In the 1980s, the situation was made worse by a war between Iran and Iraq, which lasted from 1980 to 1988. In Western countries, it took a long time for awareness of the Iranian refugee problem to develop.

Many of the Iranians who fled joined family members who already lived in the United States or Canada. Some expected to return to Iran when the political situation there improved and the government became less repressive. But in the Islamic Republic of Iran, Muslim clerics are guaranteed significant power, and they enforce a conservative interpretation of Islam that limits personal freedoms. After the Ayatollah Khomeini died in 1989, he was replaced as Supreme Leader by the Ayatollah Ali Khamenei, who was still in power as of 2016. Human rights organizations have consistently documented widespread abuses by the Iranian government.

Life for the Iranian Refugee

Canada and the United States have welcomed many Iranians. In 1982, Canada announced that it was creating a special program for Iranian refugees. Canada admitted about 500 Iranian refugees that year, and another 500 in 1983. The refugee program concentrated on assisting Baha'is, and members of the religion raised money to help the refugees travel to and get settled in their new country. In the decades that followed, Canada continued to accept Baha'is, as well as other Iranian refugees. In 2014, according to Citizenship and Immigration Canada, Iran ranked as the third-largest source country for refugees admitted into Canada.

From 1980 through 2013, approximately 275,000 Iranians immigrated to the United States. The number of Iranians admitted as refugees averaged about 3,100 annually from 2004 to 2013.

In the United States today, the largest Iranian communities are in Los Angeles, San Francisco, New York, and Washington, D.C. Southern California has the highest Iranian population in the world outside of Iran itself. Some estimates say that there are as many as 600,000 Iranians in this area. Iranians in Los Angeles like to call the city "Tehrangeles" after Tehran, Iran's capital city. The average Iranian in the United States earns more money and has more education than the average American. Many Iranians have had a lot of success in the business world.

The American-Iranian community is interested in preserving its cultural identity. In the United States, there are many Iranian newspapers and magazines, radio stations, and cultural organizations. In California alone, there are almost 40 of these special organizations. Along with maintaining their cultural pride, Iranians have also pursued an American identity. Sanam Ansari, the president of the Iranian Students Group at the University of California, noted: "They have a word in Persian, 'do-hava.' It means 'two-weathered.' You're not completely American and not completely Iranian." At the same time, Iranians have had to face prejudice. Ever since the Iranian hostage crisis, some Americans have associated Iran with terrorism and anti-Americanism; however, since Iranian refugees are typically not Muslim, this problem has affected them less than it has the general Iranian immigrant community.

Canada has large Iranian communities in several cities, including Montreal and Vancouver. In Vancouver, there are nearly 30,000 Iranians from different religious backgrounds, including the Muslim, Baha'i, Jewish, Zoroastrian, and Christian faiths. The Persian newspaper *Shahrvand-e-Vancouver* (in Persian, "Citizens of Vancouver") has a weekly circulation of 10,000 around Canada. Vancouver is a city whose residents have come from all over the world, and for many different reasons. Some Iranians say that the beautiful scenery surrounding Vancouver has drawn them to the city, especially the mountains of North Vancouver, which remind them of the mountains of Tehran.

Other Middle Eastern Refugees

Iranian refugees and immigrants are far from being the only Middle Eastern people to have come in large numbers to North

Syrian children in a refugee camp in Turkey. Since a civil war began in Syria during 2011, millions of people have fled from the fighting. In 2016, U.S. President Barack Obama encouraged the government to accept at least 10,000 Syrian refugees.

America. Particularly in the United States, there are communities that have welcomed people from different Middle Eastern countries for over a century. One of these communities is Detroit, Michigan, and its surrounding suburbs, especially Dearborn. In the beginning of the 20th century, these communities became centers for Henry Ford's car production company.

Middle Eastern immigrants have been arriving in the United States since the 1870s. Many Middle Eastern laborers—a majority of them Lebanese men—found employment with Ford and other companies during the car manufacturing boom. Michigan's Middle Eastern community was well established before World War II.

Since the end of that war, the Middle East has witnessed continual turmoil. Much of it has been fueled by the Arab-Israeli conflict.

In 1947, the United Nations adopted a resolution to partition Palestine into a Jewish state and a Palestinian Arab state. But while the Jewish people accepted the partition plan, the Palestinians did not. And after the State of Israel was proclaimed on May 14, 1948, Israel's Arab neighbors Egypt, Jordan, Syria, Lebanon, and Iraq attacked. By early 1949, Israel had defeated the combined armies of the Arab countries and taken much of the land the UN had allocated for a Palestinian state. Jordan and Egypt took the rest. Palestinians were left with no land of their own. In 1967, Israel fought another war, with Egypt, Syria, and Jordan. Again the Israelis triumphed.

In 1978 and again in 1982, Israel invaded Lebanon in order to stop Palestinian terrorist incursions from that country. Lebanon was in the midst of its own brutal civil war, which lasted from 1975 to 1990.

In August 1990, as the Lebanese civil war was nearing an end, Iraqi dictator Saddam Hussein ordered his army to invade Kuwait, Iraq's southern neighbor. Early the following year, an international coalition formed under the authority of the UN and spearheaded by the United States expelled Iraqi forces from Kuwait in what came to be called the Gulf War.

These Middle Eastern conflicts, and others, produced large numbers of refugees. Many of these refugees came to North America. Among those who entered the United States, a significant portion gravitated to the Detroit area—which wasn't surprising, given that an Arab American community was already well established there. In the decade after the end of the 1991 Gulf War, for example, an average of about 3,000 Iraqi refugees per year settled in or around Detroit.

Another war would eventually lead to much greater numbers of Iraqi refugees being admitted into the United States. In 2002, President George W. Bush and members of his administration began asserting that Iraq hadn't abided by cease-fire terms imposed at the conclusion of the Gulf War. Specifically, the Bush administration claimed, Iraq had failed to get rid of its chemical and biological weapons and was trying to develop nuclear weapons. Additionally, the administration implied that the Iraqi regime had ties with al-Qaeda, which had carried out the terrorist attacks of September 11, 2001. All of those claims would turn out to be unfounded. But in March 2003 the United States launched an invasion of Iraq, and Saddam Hussein's dictatorial regime was quickly toppled. However, in the months and years that followed, Iraq descended into chaos, with Iraq's Sunni and Shia Muslims battling each other, and with Sunnis and foreign terrorist groups fighting American occupation forces.

Iraqis who helped the Americans (for example, by serving as interpreters) were especially vulnerable to reprisals, yet the United States was slow to take them as refugees. Through 2006, a total of about 500 Iraqi refugees had been resettled in the United States. The pace accelerated in 2007, when the United States admitted about 1,600 Iraqi refugees, and took off in 2008, when close to 14,000 were admitted. In the years that followed, the numbers remained high; about 19,500 Iraqi refugees came to the United States in 2013. By then the United States had resettled more than 100,000 Iraqi refugees in all.

Canada, too, did its part to aid Iraq's refugees. It accepted more than 20,000 Iraqi refugees from 2013 to 2015.

By then, a massive new refugee crisis was under way. Syria's civil war had created more than 4.5 million refugees. Canada pledged to accept 10,000 over a three-year period.

President Barack Obama called for the United States to resettle at least 10,000 Syrian refugees in 2016. But Republican members of Congress vowed to prevent that, citing concerns that terrorists might gain entry into the country by posing as Syrian refugees.

 # Text-Dependent Questions

1. Identify at least two reasons the shah of Iran was unpopular with his people.
2. Name two Canadian cities that have large Iranian communities.
3. Which new country was proclaimed on May 14, 1948?

 # Research Project

The Middle East's three major religions—Judaism, Christianity, and Islam—all consider Jerusalem a holy city. Find out why.

6 REFUGEES FROM EUROPE

Europe has seen millions of people become refugees and displaced persons within its borders, a significant portion of them a result of the two world wars. In the decades since the end of World War II, there have been other refugee movements within Europe, many starting in the Soviet Union and Eastern Europe. People have been forced to leave their countries because of the violent rise and fall of governments, political and religious persecution, or fighting between ethnic groups.

In the 1990s, crises in Yugoslavia quickly created some of the largest refugee movements in history. In many cases, the people displaced by these conflicts have fled to other countries in Europe. The United States and Canada have also played important roles in helping these refugees by moving them to safer places and resettling them temporarily or permanently.

Hungarian and Czechoslovakian Refugees

In the 1950s, the Soviet Union maintained control over the countries of Eastern Europe. There was very little political and religious freedom under the communist governments of these countries. Freedom of information was also limited. It was illegal to own or produce books and other publications that indi-

◀ A group of Hungarian refugees walk along a snowy road soon after crossing the border into Yugoslavia, March 1957. They were among the hundreds of thousands who fled Hungary after a Soviet invasion. Some of these refugees were welcomed by countries that opposed the spread of communism, including the United States and Canada.

cated or supported an anti-communist perspective. In Hungary, revolutionaries overthrew the Soviet-backed government in October 1956 and attempted to set up their own government in its place. The revolution lasted for only a week. On November 4, the Soviet army entered the Hungarian capital and crushed the uprising.

Over the next few months, hundreds of thousands of Hungarians fled the country. Many of them went to Austria and other European countries. Partly because of their anti-communist policies, the United States and Canada also welcomed many of the Hungarian refugees. During the crisis, the United States accepted over 38,000 of the refugees, and for the first time, the government gave cash assistance to voluntary agencies to help these refugees resettle. Most of them were resettled in New York, New Jersey, Pennsylvania, and Ohio, where there were already many Hungarian immigrants.

There was some concern that a few of the Hungarian refugees might be communist spies, but the U.S. government still set aside rigid quota restrictions so that the refugees could enter the country in large numbers. A report by Vice President Richard Nixon to President Dwight Eisenhower said of the Hungarian refugees: "The large majority are young people—students, technicians, craftsmen and professional people." People with these skills were viewed as valuable additions to the United States. Nixon's report also stated:

> For the most part they were in the forefront of the fight for freedom. . . . The majority of the refugees who have been interviewed say that they left Hungary because of fear of liquidation

 Words to Understand in This Chapter

anti-Semitism—hostility toward or hatred of Jewish people as a group.

bloc—a group of countries that are connected by a treaty or agreement or by common goals.

refusenik—a Jew refused permission to emigrate from the Soviet Union.

or of deportation. The number of [communist] floaters and of those who left Hungary purely for economic reasons is relatively small.

The Canadian government accepted over 37,000 refugees resulting from the Hungarian crisis. A greater percentage of the Hungarian refugee population went to Canada than to the United States or any other country. As in the United States, there had been fears among Canadians that Soviet spies would enter the country with the refugees. Nonetheless, during the crisis the Canadian government changed its policy of accepting limited numbers of refugees from Soviet-controlled countries. J. W. Pickersgill, Minister of Immigration at the time, set up a Hungarian Immigration Branch and advised the Canadian officials dealing with the refugees: "Unless your Security Officer has serious reason to believe the applicant is a security risk, we would expect him to issue a security clearance."

Some of those fleeing Hungary were Jews, a group that had not been heartily accepted by Canada in the past. With the Hungarian crisis, though, Canadians started to overcome their prejudices against Jewish refugees. The Canadian federal government was mainly responsible for resettling the refugees, providing them with education, and helping them to find work. But the refugees also received help from voluntary organizations, universities, provincial governments, and private sponsors. As in the United States, most of the Hungarian refugees stayed permanently in Canada.

In 1968, Czechoslovakia faced a similar situation to that of Hungary in 1956. During the "Prague Spring," Czechoslovakia's leader tried to establish a more liberal socialist government in place of the very restrictive regimes that were the norm in Soviet-controlled Eastern Europe. Soviet troops quickly invaded and violently put an end to the experiment in "socialism with a human face." Compared to the departure of refugees after the Hungarian revolution, much fewer refugees left the country after the Prague Spring. Canada accepted about 12,000 of the Czechoslovakian refugees. Their communist background was no longer considered much of a problem. Instead, the Canadian government looked at the refugees as valuable additions to the workforce, since most of them were young, well educated, and had the skills that employers needed. The refugees settled in different parts of Canada, with large clusters in provinces such as Ontario, Alberta, and British Columbia.

Jewish Refugees from the Soviet Union

The Soviet Union didn't permit large-scale emigration. People who wanted to leave the country were often seen as traitors. In many cases, those who applied for an exit visa were immediately fired from their job; occasionally they would be committed to a mental institution.

In the Soviet Union (as in Russia before it), anti-Semitism was widespread. After the 1967 Six Day War, in which Israel defeated the Soviet Union's Arab allies Egypt and Syria, hostility toward Soviet Jews increased. It was fanned by the Soviet government. Many Soviet Jews began asking for permission to emigrate, but very few applications were granted. Jews denied the exit visas they sought were known as "refuseniks."

In 1971, however, the Soviet government reversed course and began granting exit visas to significant numbers of refuseniks. Jews began leaving the country in large numbers. Israel was the traditional destination for this group, but many, especially those who were younger and less devoted to the Jewish faith, chose to move to the United States instead. In 1979, a peak year for departures, over 51,000 Jews left the Soviet Union. Almost two-thirds of them went to the United States.

The dispute over the free emigration of Soviet Jews became a major part of U.S.-Soviet summits and the overall topic of dialogue between the two countries. After the United States protested the Soviet invasion of Afghanistan in 1979, and provided military aid to Afghan rebels, one of the Soviet's government responses was to again severely restrict the number of Jews permitted to leave the country each year. The thaw in U.S.-Soviet relations after Mikhail Gorbachev became Soviet leader in 1985 eventually helped restart the the next wave of emigrating Soviet Jews.

It was common for some Jews to leave the Soviet Union with entry papers for Israel, but to change destinations along the way and go to the United States. The Israeli government feared that if the United States continued to accept Jewish refugees who migrated in this manner, the Soviet government might start preventing them from emigrating. During the late 1980s, Russian Jews continued to leave the Soviet Union. Many of them were still choosing the United States as their final destination, but by this time, the process was better regulated, and they could apply directly to the U.S. government for entry. In the 1990s, an increasing number of evangelical Christians also became refugees based on their fear of religious persecution in the former Soviet Union. Between 1988 and 2001, more than 460,000 refugees from the former Soviet Union came to the United States.

Refugees of the Balkans

During that same period, some of the worst refugee crises in history arose on southeastern Europe's Balkan Peninsula. Those crises came about as the Socialist Federal Republic of Yugoslavia disintegrated.

Yugoslavia—initially called the Kingdom of Serbs, Croats, and Slovenes—was formed in the aftermath of World War I. Much of its territory came from the defeated Austro-Hungarian Empire. Yugoslavia was torn apart during World War II.

After that war, it was re-formed as a communist state modeled on the lines of the Soviet Union (though Yugoslavia would split with the Soviet bloc in 1948 and remain nonaligned thereafter). Yugoslavia was made up of six "socialist republics": Bosnia and Herzegovina, Croatia, Macedonia, Montenegro, Serbia, and Slovenia. Serbia, the largest of the socialist republics, was home to the national capital, Belgrade. It also contained two autonomous provinces, Kosovo and Vojvodina.

Yugoslavia's people came from various ethnic groups (some of which had been in conflict in the past) and professed different religious creeds. But the country was held together by communism, and by the force of will of its leader, Josip Broz Tito.

Tito died in 1980, though, and by 1989 communist regimes were collapsing throughout Eastern Europe. In Yugoslavia, nationalism began bubbling up.

Slobodan Milosevic, the president of Serbia, inflamed the passions of ethnic Serbs, who are Orthodox Christians, against the Muslim, ethnic Albanian people of Kosovo. In 1989 Milosevic spearheaded constitutional changes that dramatically reduced the Kosovo province's political autonomy. He also championed measures that put many Kosovars (Kosovo Albanians) out of work. Riots ensued. When leaders in Slovenia and Croatia announced their support for the Kosovars, angry demonstrations erupted in Serbia denouncing the Slovenian and Croatian leaders.

On June 25, 1991, Slovenia and Croatia both declared their independence from Yugoslavia. After a brief war, the Yugoslavian government implicitly acceded to Slovenia's independence in order to concentrate on fighting the much larger Croatia. In Croatia, a Serb minority declared its desire to unite with Serbia. Serb militias joined with the Serb-controlled Yugoslavian national army to battle Croatian forces. The fighting was pitiless, with horrible atrocities committed by both sides.

Macedonia declared its independence in late 1991. Thankfully, no bloodshed occurred there.

The same could not be said of Bosnia and Herzegovina. In a referendum held in early 1992, people in that socialist republic voted for independence from Yugoslavia. But Bosnia and Herzegovina's Serbs rejected the referendum and announced their own independent state, the Republika Srpska. Its army, along with the Yugoslavian national army, waged a merciless war against Bosnia and Herzegovina's Muslims (or Bosniaks) and ethnic Croats (some of whom also formed a self-proclaimed Croat state). The Serb forces became notorious for what they euphemistically referred to as "ethnic cleansing": clearing areas of the other ethnic groups through the forced expulsion or wholesale slaughter of civilians.

Throughout the various conflicts, the United Nations sent

Muslim refugees wait line to receive food rations at a temporary UN housing facility in Croatia, 1992.

UNHCR relief workers and other representatives into the Balkans. Although UNHCR tried to help the victims of violence, it could do little to stop the ethnic cleansing and fighting. From 1992 to 1996, UNHCR organized an ongoing airlift into the Balkans. Airplanes brought food, medicine, and supplies to Sarajevo, the capital of Bosnia, which was the scene of some of the worst fighting. Many of the airplanes came from the United States and Canada.

Beginning in the mid-1990s, thousands of refugees were resettled in the United States and Canada. By 2013, the United States alone had accepted about 169,000. The United States took 38,000 refugees from Bosnia and Herzegovina during and after the war years. Canada took the same number of refugees from Bosnia and Herzegovina and other countries in the region. About 30 percent of these refugees were children, many of whom continued to suffer from the memories of what they had experienced. In one U.S. school, young Bosnian refugees were asked to draw pictures of home. One student drew a picture of himself standing in front of men with guns, over which he wrote in his native Serbo-Croatian: "I was dreaming how they shot me." Despite their hardships, many Bosnians found that they could adjust to their new countries and make a fresh start with their families.

In the United States, Chicago and St. Louis have the largest Bosnian populations. Before 1993, St. Louis did not have a large population of refugees. By 2002, the Bosnian population in the city had grown to around 40,000, and a similar number lived in Chicago. Some Bosnians moved to communities that were much smaller. In the town of Bowling Green, Kentucky, the Bosnian population had grown to 2,500 by 2001. Tatjana Sahanic, one of the newcomers, said: "The community was shocked by our arrival. They didn't know anything about us; we didn't know anything about them." Given time, though, most of them have found employment, and some have started businesses and purchased homes, becoming valued members of the community.

In 1995, a peace agreement officially ended the war in Bosnia and Herzegovina. A few years later, less than 10 percent of the people displaced by the fighting had been able to return home. Meanwhile, another crisis had arisen in Kosovo.

In February 1998, severe fighting broke out in Kosovo between Yugoslav Serbian forces and the Kosovo Liberation Army (KLA). The KLA was a military force established in 1997 to fight for the ethnic Albanians in Kosovo. Although the United Nations and other organizations tried to negotiate an end to this war, the situation had worsened by the beginning of 1999. It became clear that Yugoslav president Slobodan Milosevic and his Serbian allies had little interest in a negotiated settlement. After peace talks collapsed in March, North Atlantic Treaty Organization (NATO) forces began attacking Yugoslav targets from the air in an attempt to prevent a Serbian takeover of Kosovo.

Serbian forces responded by moving into Kosovo and

expelling as much of the Albanian population as possible. Mentor Nimani, a Kosovar Albanian human rights attorney, described the events after the Serb attack on Kosovo before the Senate Immigration Subcommittee on April 14, 1999:

> In Tirana [the capital of Albania], I began to talk to other refugees and document their stories. They spoke to me of the ordeals they had suffered and the atrocities they had witnessed. I spoke to one group of refugees from Peja [a city in Kosovo]. They told me that Serb authorities had expelled them from Kosovo and ordered them to walk to Albania. The men were separated from the women and they were threatened with death if they did not come up with money. To spare the men, the group gave the authorities all their money. On the way to Albania, two children and an elderly woman died. The group traveled without food or water. But, their worst experience was when they reached the border. There, Serb authorities forced them to stay the night. While they were trying to sleep in the open, loud speakers played. On the loud speakers they heard the voices of children screaming as if they were being killed. They also heard continuous threats of atrocities that would be committed against them, including descriptions of how they would be killed. One woman I spoke with said that this was the worst experience of her life. She will never be able to recover from this.
>
> Another man and woman from Gakova [a town in northwest Serbia] described their escape from that city. Soldiers shot at them as they fled. They believe that eighty percent of the city has been set on fire and destroyed. In one mosque they passed in Gakova as they fled, they saw as many as 300 bodies of people slain.

The NATO air campaign lasted for 78 days. It was called a "humanitarian war" because it was meant to stop the fighting on the ground, but it also made the refugee crisis even worse. After the start of the air campaign, violence against the ethnic Albanians increased. In a short period, 800,000 ethnic Albanians had fled Kosovo. Many of them headed for the Macedonian border, to the south. Soon, Macedonian officials closed the border, stating that the country could not cope at that time with such a huge wave of refugees. But when it received pressure from UNHCR and NATO, Macedonia agreed to open its borders again, but it did so on the condition that other countries would help to evacuate the Albanian refugees. These "third

countries" would accept the refugees for temporary or permanent resettlement.

About 95,000 refugees went to host countries around the world. Approximately 4,000 Kosovar Albanians were interviewed overseas and, to assure their protection, airlifted to Fort Dix in New Jersey to complete the interview process. Eventually, a total of more than Kosovar 10,000 refugees entered the United States, while more than 7,000 went to Canada. The American program that brought the refugees directly to the United States was called "Operation Provide Refuge." The U.S. government loaned money to the refugees to cover travel costs to the United States; it was decided later that this loan did not have to be paid back.

In an unprecedented move for the U.S. refugee settlement program, the government also offered to pay for any refugee's return to Kosovo after the crisis ended. The deadline for registering in the funded return program was May 1, 2000. When that date arrived, one-third of the refugees had returned to Kosovo or had applied to return.

In Canada, the refugees first went to military bases in Ontario and other eastern provinces. They were then resettled in towns and cities all over the country. For a period of two years, monthly payments from the government helped the refugees get established. Sponsorship groups gave them practical help with shopping, registering their children in schools, and finding their way around their new communities. In some cases, Canadian individuals and families took refugees into their own homes. One Canadian immigration official said of the people's attitude toward the refugees: "The next best thing to motherhood and apple pie was to have a Kosovar in your spare bedroom." By March 2000, only 1,900 of the more than 7,000 Kosovar refugees in Canada had chosen to return home. Although some were eager to go back to Kosovo as soon as possible, others decided that they wanted to stay in Canada permanently.

Many of the refugees felt that they had little to return to. They had lost their homes, their jobs, and even their friends and family members. But the welcoming attitude of most Canadians also encouraged them to stay. "I love Canada," said one refugee named Nita. "The people are very kind. I will stay here."

 # Text-Dependent Questions

1. In which four states were most Hungarian refugees accepted into the United States settled after the Hungarian revolution of 1956?

2. What was the Prague Spring?

3. To what does the term Bosniak refer?

 # Research Project

The Warsaw Pact was an alliance between the Soviet Union and Soviet-dominated communist countries of Eastern Europe. Compile a list of the Warsaw Pact members. Note which of the countries in the alliance no longer exist.

7 THE CHALLENGES AHEAD

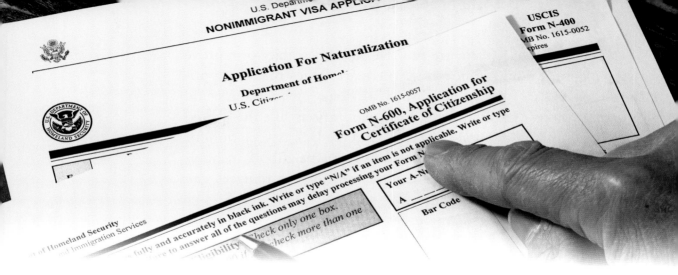

The relationship between North America and those who arrive on its shores as refugees has never been without trials. Both refugees and the people who facilitate their arrival aim to continually make the admission process easier and fairer. The United States and Canada have worked hard toward reaching their goals for refugees, and both nations are recognized as world leaders in refugee assistance.

In the United States and Canada, refugee assistance workers strive to maintain that position as international leaders. In addition to addressing particular refugee issues at home, organization leaders are often concerned with the bigger picture of how international policy affects refugees around the world. Organizations like the U.S. Refugee Committee and UNHCR address the conditions that cause refugee crises, such as poverty, civil war, and various forms of persecution. The prevention of future refugee crises rests largely on peace negotiations as well as the large-scale humanitarian efforts of organizations to redevelop destabilized countries.

◀ Filippo Grandi (left), who became UN High Commissioner for Refugees in January 2016, is pictured with UN Secretary-General Ban Ki-moon. Organizations like UNHCR and the U.S. Refugee Committee continue to offer assistance to the displaced people of the world, although their staggering numbers make such a goal very challenging.

International leaders are not the only ones able to improve the plight of refugees, however. There are things that every private citizen can do to help, such as donating to refugee aid organizations or volunteering for organizations like the United Nations Children's Fund (UNICEF) and the U.S. Association for UNHCR. Americans and Canadians with neighbors, schoolmates, workmates, and friends who were or are refugees can have an even more direct impact.

Showing an interest in refugees and their unique history is a good way to offer support. Refugees face difficulties that many typical North Americans have not faced: they have been uprooted and thrust into a society in which things such as language, culture, food, money, and even weather can be completely new and different. Newcomers may appreciate it when someone takes the time to listen to their story, or suggests ways to help them adjust to their new life.

There is no reason to assume that refugees will immediately feel at home upon resettling. It may be true that many things are better for refugees in Canada or the United States than they were in their original home, but this does not mean they will immediately leave their former lives behind. Like all immigrants, refugees are encouraged to embrace new values and appreciate cultural differences. The level of comfort they feel as North American residents is affected by how their peers appreciate those differences in return.

That refugees even exist is one of the modern world's tragedies. Instead of reaching a resolution, this problem has continued and, in certain parts of the world, worsened. The United

 Words to Understand in This Chapter

facilitate—to make something easier; to help something run more smoothly or efficiently.

peer—a person who belongs to the same age group or social group as someone else.

The Challenge for the Children

In most refugee movements, at least half of the refugees are children under the age of 18. The situation of these young people is especially sad and difficult. It is hard for them to make their voices heard and protect their basic rights. Their lives become even harder if they are separated from their parents and families, or if their parents have died. Refugee children can often be resettled with relatives or host families in new countries. Unfortunately, others end up being detained or sent back to an uncertain future in their home country.

In 1993, UNHCR adopted the Policy on Refugee Children, put forward in a document entitled "The Challenge: The Special Needs of Refugee Children." It reads: "Children, including refugee children, are the future. They need special protection and care to realize their potential." The policy focuses on keeping families together, treating all refugee children equally, and protecting the children from the risks that they may face as refugees.

When they arrive in their host countries, many refugee children suffer from physical or psychological problems that have emerged after their experiences. In some parts of the United States and Canada, there are special programs to help refugee children to feel safe and happy in their new countries. In Toronto, Canada, a school program called Building Bridges helps refugee children to talk about their problems freely, to express themselves through art, and to make new friends.

States and Canada, as well as some other countries, have taken up the challenge of helping those who have been forced to leave their homes. Everyone, from the most powerful government officials to schoolchildren, can help refugees as they adjust to the many changes and challenges that they face in their new homes.

Text-Dependent Questions

1. What does UNICEF stand for?
2. About what proportion of refugees are children and youth under the age of 18?

Research Project

To become a U.S. citizen, an immigrant from another country must pass a civics test. U.S. Citizenship and Immigration Services offers practice tests at: https://my.uscis.gov/prep/test/civics/view
Take a test. What percentage did you get correct? Do some further research about any answers you got wrong.

Series Glossary of Key Terms

assimilate—to adopt the ways of another culture; to fully become part of a different country or society.

census—an official count of a country's population.

deport—to forcibly remove someone from a country, usually back to his or her native land.

green card—a document that denotes lawful permanent resident status in the United States.

migrant laborer—an agricultural worker who travels from region to region, taking on short-term jobs.

naturalization—the act of granting a foreign-born person citizenship.

passport—a paper or book that identifies the holder as the citizen of a country; usually required for traveling to or through other foreign lands.

undocumented immigrant—a person who enters a country without official authorization; sometimes referred to as an "illegal immigrant."

visa—official authorization that permits arrival at a port of entry but does not guarantee admission into the United States.

Further Reading

Bourke, Dale Hanson. *Immigration: Tough Questions, Direct Answers.* Downers Grove, IL: InterVarsity Press, 2014.

Bradman, Tony, ed. *Give Me Shelter: Stories About Children Who Seek Asylum.* London: Frances Lincoln Children's Books, 2007.

Chomsky, Aviva. *Undocumented: How Immigration Became Illegal.* Boston: Beacon Press, 2014.

Cutts, Mark, ed. *The State of the World's Refugees, 2000: Fifty Years of Humanitarian Action.* UNHCR. New York: Oxford University Press, 2000.

Eire, Carlos. *Learning to Die in Miami: Confessions of a Refugee Boy.* New York: Simon & Schuster, 2010.

Gjelten, Tom. *A Nation of Nations: A Great American Immigration Story.* New York: Simon and Schuster, 2015.

Kenney, David Ngaruri, and Philip G. Schrag. *Asylum Denied: A Refugee's Struggle for Safety in America.* Berkeley and Los Angeles: University of California Press, 2008.

Lewin-Epstein, Noah et al., eds. *Russian Jews on Three Continents: Migration and Resettlement.* London: Frank Cass, 1997.

Loescher, Gil. *The UNHCR and World Politics: A Perilous Path.* Oxford, England: Oxford University Press, 2001.

Merino, Noel. *Illegal Immigration.* San Diego: Greenhaven Press, 2015.

Pipher, Mary. *The Middle of Everywhere: The World's Refugees Come to Our Town.* New York: Harcourt Books, 2002.

Robinson, W. Courtland. *Terms of Refuge: The Indochinese Exodus and the International Response.* New York: St Martin's Press, 1998.

Internet Resources

www.uscis.gov

The website of U.S. Citizenship and Immigration Services offers information about immigration eligibility, citizenship, and more.

www.cic.gc.ca/english/refugees/index.asp

A wealth of information about Canada's approach to refugees and asylum, from Citizenship and Immigration Canada.

www.hrw.org/topic/refugees

News, reports, and videos about refugees from Human Rights Watch.

http://refugees.org

U.S. Committee for Refugees and Immigrants. Covers refugee issues, especially as they relate to the United States, and reports on the most recent developments involving refugees.

www.unhcr.org/cgi-bin/texis/vtx/home

The home page of the United Nations High Commissioner for Refugees.

Index

1951 Convention, 22–24, 25, 42, 48
1976 Immigration Act (Canada), 40, 48
1952 Immigration and Nationality Act, 31
1965 Immigration and Nationality Act, 31–32, **34**
1967 Protocol, 23–24, 42, 48

ABC v. Meese, 63
   See also asylum
Adamkus, Valdas, 102
African refugees, 23–24
Albanians, ethnic, 91–92, 93–95
   See also Balkan refugees
Albright, Madeleine, 102
Amine, Hoda, 85
Ansari, Sanam, 83
Aristide, Jean-Bertrand, 70, 72
   See also Haiti
Ashcroft, John, 74
asylum, 42, 45, 47, 48–49, 63
   See also refugees
Austria, 20
Ayuen, Monica Tito, 15–16

Balkan refugees, 91–97
Barnes, Walter, 58
Batista, Fulgencio, **61**, 62
boat people, **51**, 55–56
   See also Indochinese refugees
Bosnia and Herzegovina, **87**, 92–93, **94**, **96**, **97**
Bureau of Citizenship and Immigration
   Services (BCIS), 35, 45–46, 47
Bureau of Customs and Border Protection
   (BCBP), 35
Bureau of Immigration and Customs
   Enforcement (BICE), 35
Bureau of Population, Refugees, and Migration
   (PRM), 45–47
Bush, George W., **35**
Califano, Joseph, 42

Cambert, Alex, 74–75
Cambodia, 51, 55, 58, 59
   See also Indochinese refugees
Canada, 17, 20, 25, 32–33, 56, 63, 83
   African refugees, 23
   Balkan refugees, 96–97
   immigration history, 38–41
   Indochinese refugees, 58–59
   refugee acceptance rate, 27–28, 51,
      54, 81, 93
   refugee policy, 41–42, 48–49, 88–89,
      99–101
Caplan, Elinor, 48
Cartagena Declaration (1984), 24–25
Carter, Jimmy, 66
del Castillo, Siro, 66–67
Castro, Fidel, **61**, 62, 64–66, 74–75
   See also Cuba
Central America, 24–25, 63
Chinese Exclusion Act of 1882, 28
   See also ethnicity
civil war, 15–16, 17, **24**, 25, 63
Clarkson, Adrienne, 49, 102
Clinton, Bill, 71
communism, 31, 39, 52–53, 62, 69, 71, 87–88, **89**
Comprehensive Plan of Action for Indo-
   Chinese Refugees (CPA), 57
      See also Indochinese refugees
Convention Governing the Specific Aspects of
   Refugee Problems in Africa, 24
Convention Relating to the Status of Refugees.
   See Geneva Convention Relating to the
   Status of Refugees (1951)
Cuba, 61–62, 64–66, 69, 71
   See also Cuban refugees
Cuban Adjustment Act, 68–69
   See also Cuban refugees
Cuban refugees, 61–62, 64–67, 68–69, 71–75
Czechoslovakia, 48, 89–90

Numbers in ***bold italic*** refer to captions.

Contributors

Senior consulting editor STUART ANDERSON is an adjunct scholar at the Cato Institute and executive director of the National Foundation for American Policy. From August 2001 to January 2003, he served as executive associate commissioner for Policy and Planning and Counselor to the Commissioner at the Immigration and Naturalization Service. He spent four and a half years on Capitol Hill on the Senate Immigration Subcommittee, first for Senator Spencer Abraham and then as Staff Director of the subcommittee for Senator Sam Brownback. Prior to that, Stuart was Director of Trade and Immigration Studies at the Cato Institute, where he produced reports on the military contributions of immigrants and the role of immigrants in high technology. Stuart has published articles in the Wall Street Journal, New York Times, Los Angeles Times, and other publications. He has an M.A. from Georgetown University and a B.A. in Political Science from Drew University. His articles have appeared in such publications as the *Wall Street Journal*, *New York Times*, and *Los Angeles Times*.

MARIAN L. SMITH served as the senior historian of the U.S. Immigration and Naturalization Service (INS) from 1988 to 2003, and is currently the immigration and naturalization historian within the Department of Homeland Security in Washington, D.C. She studies, publishes, and speaks on the history of the immigration agency and is active in the management of official 20th-century immigration records.

PETER HAMMERSCHMIDT is director general of national cyber security at Public Safety Canada. He previously served as First Secretary (Financial and Military Affairs) for the Permanent Mission of Canada to the United Nations. Before taking this position, he was a ministerial speechwriter and policy specialist for the Department of National Defence in Ottawa. Prior to joining the public service, he served as the Publications Director for the Canadian Institute of Strategic Studies in Toronto. He has a B.A. (Honours) in Political Studies from Queen's University, and an MScEcon in Strategic Studies from the University of Wales, Aberystwyth.

MIKE VENETTONE is a freelance writer and editor. A native of Philadelphia, he currently lives in New York City with his wife and three children. This is his first book.

Picture Credits